Wall mural, Healdsburg, California

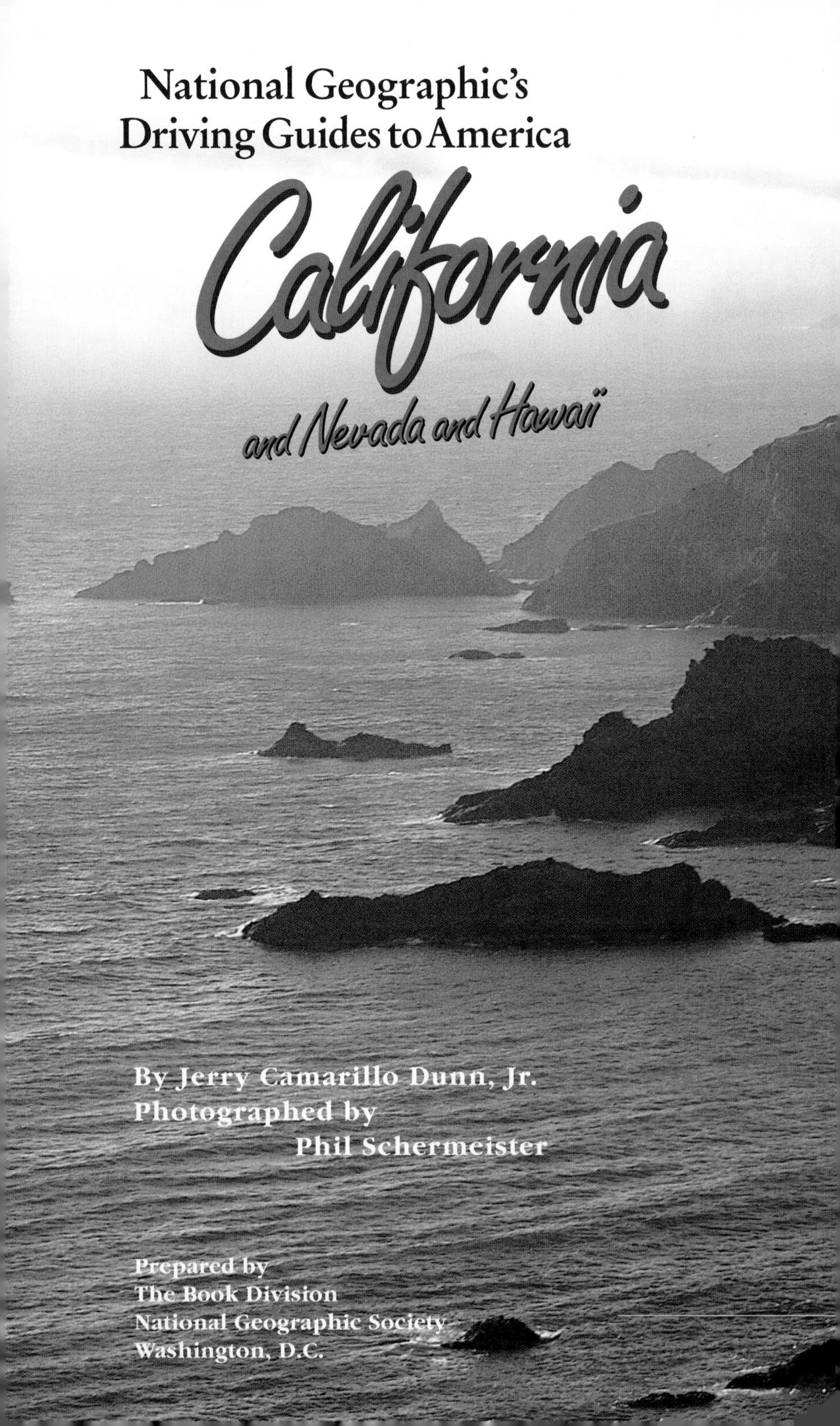

National Geographic's
Driving Guides to America

California

and Nevada and Hawaii

By Jerry Camarillo Dunn, Jr.
Photographed by
Phil Schermeister

Prepared by
The Book Division
National Geographic Society
Washington, D.C.

**National Geographic's
Driving Guides To America
California and Nevada and Hawaii**

By Jerry Camarillo Dunn, Jr.
Photographed by Phil Schermeister

Published by
The National Geographic Society

Reg Murphy
President and Chief Executive Officer
Gilbert M. Grosvenor
Chairman of the Board
Nina D. Hoffman
Senior Vice President

Prepared by The Book Division
William R. Gray
Vice President and Director
Charles Kogod
Assistant Director
Barbara A. Payne
Editorial Director

Driving Guides to America
Elizabeth L. Newhouse
*Director of Travel Books
and Series Editor*
Cinda Rose
Art Director
Thomas B. Powell III
Illustrations Editor
Caroline Hickey, Barbara A. Noe
Senior Researchers
Carl Mehler
Map Editor and Designer

Staff for this book
Barbara A. Noe
Editor
Jody Bolt Littlehales
Designer
Thomas B. Powell III
Illustrations Editor
Mary Luders, K. M. Kostyal
Contributing Editors

Sean M. Groom
Michael H. Higgins
Mary E. Jennings
Keith R. Moore
Daniel M. Nonte
Researchers

Paulette Claus
Copy Editor

Thomas L. Gray, Louis J. Spirito,
Tracey M. Wood
Map Researchers
Michelle H. Picard, Louis J. Spirito,
Martin S. Walz, Tracey M. Wood
Map Production
Tibor G. Tóth
Map Relief

Meredith Wilcox
Illustrations Assistant

Richard S. Wain
Production Project Manager
Lewis R. Bassford, Lyle Rosbotham
Production

Rhonda Brown, Kevin G. Craig,
Dale M. Herring, Peggy Purdy,
Robert Weatherly
Staff Assistants

Elisabeth MacRae-Bobynskyj
Indexer

Suez Kehl, Robert Weatherly, Joan
Wolbier
Contributors

**Manufacturing
and Quality Management**
George V. White
Director
John T. Dunn
Associate Director
Vincent P. Ryan
Manager

Cover: Golden Gate Bridge,
San Francisco, Calif.

Previous pages: Along Calif. 1
near Jenner

Facing page: Kona coast at sunset,
Hawaii

OREGON   IDAHO

REDWOOD
N.P.

96

**Redwood
Country** ★
★★

101 Eureka   89   **The** ★
36   **Cascades**

3   5

101   LASSEN
                                          VOLCANIC
36   N.P.

Redding

89   395

Fort
Bragg   5   **Mother**
                        Lode   89
North ★   **and the**   445   Reno
Coast   **Sierra**   **Carson City**
                        ★★   Lake   50
                               Tahoe **Lake Tahoe and**
1   101 **Sacramento**   **the Comstock** ★★

Napa Valley ★★   80   50
and the
Pacific   4
San
Francisco   49   YOSEMITE
                               N.P.   6
                                         Great Parks
San Francisco ★   San Jose   99   ★★
Bay Area
            Santa Cruz   CALIFORNIA   95
            Monterey   41   KINGS
                                 CANYON
                        Fresno 180 N.P. 395   DEATH
                                               VALLEY
                        198   SEQUOIA   190 N.P.
Central   65   N.P.   395
Coast   155
★★   1   5   178
         San Luis
         Obispo   127

Santa ★   **Los Angeles**   15
Barbara   **to the**
Loop   **Mountains**   40
         Santa Barbara
         CHANNEL   101
         ISLANDS   **Los Angeles**   15
         N.P.
                        Disneyland   62   JOSHUA
                        and the Beaches   TREE N.P.
         Santa Catalina Island   15   86   Salton 10
                                         Sea
Kauai ★★   **San Diego**   78
Kauai   **Ramble**
     Lihue   San Diego   8   U.S.
Niihau   MEXICO

NEVADA

Elko   80

278 **Northeastern** ★
     Frontier
                93
50   Ely
                GREAT
                BASIN N.P.
6

95

93

Las Vegas
Recreational
Pursuits
Las Vegas ★
                Lake
                Mead

                ARIZONA

                95

Oahu **Oahu**
Honolulu

     Molokai
         Kahului
Lanai   **Maui** ★
Kahoolawe HALEAKALA N.P.
         Maui

H A W A I I

                ★★ Hilo
     Kailua **Hawaii**
     Hawaii
                HAWAII
                VOLCANOES N.P.

6

Contents

Good Company 8
About the Guides 9

California

Redwood Country *10*
The Cascades *18*
North Coast *26*
Napa Valley and the Pacific *32*
San Francisco Bay Area *40*
Central Coast *50*
Santa Barbara Loop *58*
Los Angeles to the Mountains *64*
Disneyland and the Beaches *72*
San Diego Ramble *76*
Great Parks *86*
Mother Lode and the Sierra *96*

Nevada

Lake Tahoe and the Comstock........*106*
Northeastern Frontier *112*
Las Vegas Recreational Pursuits *118*

Hawaii

Oahu *124*
Kauai *132*
Maui *140*
Hawaii *148*

For More Information *156*
*Notes on Author
 and Photographer* *156*
Index *157*

One thing I liked about traveling all over the Far West was that I had such good company. Mark Twain, Robert Louis Stevenson, and other writers once wandered the same trails, scattering their words like bread crumbs to follow.

In 1864 Twain wryly observed a Nevada that still exists today: "The country looks something like a singed cat . . . in the respect that it has more merits than its personal appearance would seem to indicate." If Twain was hinting at surprises, I found some. Late one afternoon, I stopped to examine boulders carved with mysterious petroglyphs. As I stood there, the darkening air exploded, and a military jet screamed past, flying low above the sagebrush. At that instant, five thousand years of human history were telescoped into an unforgettable scene. And this was just one of Nevada's hidden surprises.

Surfers at Sandy Beach Park, Oahu, Hawaii

8

Open Roads

Driving in California is reasonably safe, with good roads everywhere—though some motorists view the speed limit (65 mph) as only a suggestion. No state has more diverse terrain, so be prepared—i.e., check your air-conditioning before you get to Death Valley. On Nevada highways you might not see another car for an hour; your only worry may be highway hypnosis. In Hawaii you potter along green country roads, and no one seems to be in much of a hurry. Not a bad way to travel. Happy Trails!

Later I headed west to California, where John Steinbeck roamed in 1962 with his dog, Charley. The writer called San Francisco "this gold and white acropolis rising wave on wave against the blue of the Pacific sky." One morning I shared his vision. Morning sun touched the city's tiers of houses, causing each facade to stand out as clearly as a temple in Greek sunlight. For a moment the city became a living Steinbeck paragraph.

Finally, I traveled about as far west as you can go in the United States—to Hawaii. In 1866 an astonished Mark Twain watched a Hawaiian surfing on a long wooden plank. "It did not seem that a lightning express train could shoot along at a more hair-lifting speed," Twain wrote. About 130 years later I'd see for myself, on Oahu's famous North Shore. Winter waves rose 25 feet high, and their crashing spattered my windshield with salty droplets. Surfers rode those moving walls of water; as I watched, Twain's words rolled down the years and broke onto that same beach.

Everywhere in the Far West, I felt the presence of earlier writers. They were great travel companions. I hope you find this book to be good company, too.

JERRY DUNN

*N*ATIONAL GEOGRAPHIC'S DRIVING GUIDES TO AMERICA invite you on memorable road trips through the United States and Canada. Intended both as travel planners and companions, each volume guides you on preplanned tours over a wide variety of terrain to the best places to see and things to do. The authors, expert regional travel writers, star-rate (from none to two ★★) the drives and points of interest to make sure you don't miss their favorites.

All distances and drive times are approximate (if you linger, as you should, plan on considerably more time). Recommended seasons are the best times to go, but roads and sites are open all year unless otherwise noted. Besides the stated days of operation, many sites close on national holidays. For the most up-to-date site information, it's best to call ahead when possible.

Then, with this book and a road map, set off on your adventure through this awesomely beautiful land.

Liberace Museum, Las Vegas, Nev.

9

MAP KEY and ABBREVIATIONS

National Conservation Area	N.C.A.	**Featured Drive**
National Monument	NAT. MON., N.M.	**Interstate Highway**
National Park	NAT. PARK., N.P.	
National Recreation Area	N.R.A.	〔5〕
National Seashore	NAT. SEASHORE	
		U.S. Federal Highway
Forest		〔101〕
Forest and Game Reserve		
Forest Reserve	FOR. RES., F.R.	**State Road**
National Forest	NAT. FOR., N.F.	〔3〕
Wilderness		
National Wildlife Refuge	N.W.R.	**County, Local, or Mexican Federal Road**
		〔2〕
State Beach	S.B.	
State Park	S.P.	**National Scenic Trail, Trail**
State Recreation Area	S.R.A.	
		State or National Border
Indian Reservation	I.R.	

Boundaries

WILDERNESS   NAT. PARK
F.R. / N.F.

Intermittent   Dry   Swamp
Lake   Lake

■ Point of Interest

★ State Capital

‖ Dam   )(Pass

+ Elevation, Peak   = Falls

ADDITIONAL ABBREVIATIONS

Fk.	*Fork*
FWY.	*Freeway*
H.S.	*Historic Site*
I.	*Island*
Jct.	*Junction*
MEM. HWY.	*Memorial Highway*
Mt.-s.	*Mountain-s, Mount*
N.H.P.	*National Historical Park*
N.H.S.	*National Historic Site*
Pk.	*Peak*
Ra.	*Range*
S.H.M	*State Historic Monument*
S.H.P.	*State Historic-al Park*
S.H.S.	*State Historic Site*
S.R.	*State Reserve*
STATE MON., S. MON.	*State Monument*
S.V.R.A.	*State Vehicular Recreation Area*
S.W.P.	*State Wayside Park*

POPULATION

● **San Francisco**	500,000 and over
● **Salinas**	50,000 to under 500,000
● **Fullerton**	under 50,000

Redwood Country★★

● **429 miles** ● **3 to 6 days** ● **Spring through fall** ● **The road from O'Brien, Oregon, to Happy Camp, California, closes in winter. Instead, follow the longer, year-round route via US 199 and I-5.**

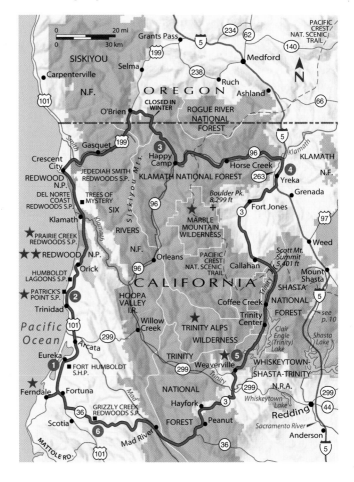

This long loop heads north out of Eureka, the north coast's largest city, and runs through the Redwood Empire, that rugged realm where groves of ancient trees rise through a heavenly cloud of fog, and eternity seems to hover like a saint among the cathedral columns. The route arches briefly into Oregon before returning to California. South past the muscular Marble Mountains and Trinity Alps, the road comes to the gold rush town of Weaverville. Finally it sweeps back to the coast, with a dainty pause at the Victorian gingerbread village of Ferndale.

Founded in 1850, **①** **Eureka** *(Chamber of Commerce 707-442-3738 or 800-356-6381)* has lived a boom-and-bust story, with chapters on mining and lumbering, shipping and fishing. Its **Old Town** *(1st to 3rd Sts. between C and M Sts.)* shows off Victorian residences and cast-iron commercial buildings of the 19th century. Point your camera (everyone else does!) at the turreted, elaborately painted, gingerbread-doodaded **Carson Mansion**★ *(2nd and M Sts. Private).* The 1885 residence of lumber baron William Carson took a hundred workers more than two years to build. Materials include redwood and stained glass, and architecture buffs will discern a mix of Queen Anne, Stick/Eastlake, and Italianate styles.

Carson Mansion, Eureka

Down the street, the **Romano Gabriel Sculpture Garden** *(317 2nd St.)* dazzles the eye. Created in the mid-20th century by an Italian gardener (and originally located in his front yard), the brightly painted trees, flowers, and human faces were sawed from vegetable crates. Look closely; this "naive" work reveals the artist's take on society, such as his disaffection for the Pope.

The nearby **Clarke Memorial Museum** *(240 E St. 707-443-1947. Tues.-Sat.; donation)* exhibits an outstanding basket collection, Indian dance costumes, pioneer firearms, a Victorian parlor, and other memorabilia. At the south end of town lies **Fort Humboldt State Historic Park** *(3431 Fort Ave. 707-445-6567),* site of an 1853 fort built after run-ins between Indians and settlers. The hospital still stands, containing a museum, and the surgeon's quarters have been reconstructed.

From the north side of town, take the bridge to the Samoa Peninsula and join the happy eaters at **Samoa Cookhouse** *(Samoa Rd. 707-442-1659),* the last logger's cookhouse in the West, built in 1892.

At the country fair, Arcata

US 101 leads north to **Arcata** *(Chamber of Commerce, 1062 G St. 707-822-3619),* home of Humboldt State University, and a hotbed of backwoods activism and ecology. Students hang out at cafés near the plaza, which is a neighborhood of historic buildings *(walking guide available at chamber).* The **Humboldt State University Natural History Museum** *(1315 G St. 707-826-4479. Tues.-Sat.)*

11

houses the impressive Maloney Fossil Collection and is worth a visit.

Reclaimed from a dump on the south edge of town, the **Arcata Marsh and Wildlife Sanctuary** *(569 S. G St. 707-822-8184. For current information on birding here and in the region, call the "birdbox" at 707-822-LOON)* shelters 200 species of birds, including waterfowl, fish eaters, and shorebirds.

Trinidad Harbor

Following the coast north, US 101 travels past beaches and the fishing village of Trinidad to ❷ **Patrick's Point State Park** ★ *(707-677-3570. Adm. fee).* Watch for passing whales from its rocky bluffs *(Nov.-Jan., March-May),* or hunt for surf-polished agate and California jade on the beach. In springtime, wander meadows that come spectacularly to life with orchids, foxgloves, and poppies.

Miles of pristine beaches await at **Humboldt Lagoons State Park** *(707-488-2041. Adm. fee),* where marshes prove popular with migrating birds, meadows with Roosevelt elk, and picnic spots with roving motorists. Surf and lagoon fishing yield perch, steelhead, and trout.

US 101 now enters **Redwood National Park** ★★ *(Visitor Center, 1 mile S of Orick. 707-464-6101).* The national park incorporates three state parks: Prairie Creek, Del Norte Coast, and Jedediah Smith. Together they protect the tallest living things on earth—redwood trees—and more than a thousand different plants and animals, from huckleberries to black bears. The best way to appreciate the trees is to get out of the car and walk among them. Enter a grove as you would a shrine where ancient mysteries abide. As you stand in the silent sanctuary, with shafts of sunlight slanting through the temple columns and your hand touching the rough bark, recall Henry David Thoreau's words: "Methinks my own soul must be a bright invisible green."

Lady Bird Johnson Grove has a 1-mile nature trail among these towering giants. Three miles farther along Bald Hills Road, **Redwood Creek Overlook** makes obvious the unhappy difference between the selective harvesting of trees and the ravages of clear-cutting. A 1.3-mile (one-way) hike descends the steep trail to Redwood Creek and the **Tall**

Trees Grove ★ *(Free permit required from Orick Visitor Center),* where one of the world's tallest trees soars 367.8 feet from alluvial flats in a bend of the creek.

At **Prairie Creek Redwoods State Park** ★ *(707-488-2171. Use fee),* herds of Roosevelt elk loll on Elk Prairie and by the dunes at Gold Bluffs Beach. Enjoy the 70-plus miles of trails that wind through redwoods, beaches, and canyons, including Fern Canyon, festooned with cool green garlands.

Just past the village of Klamath, detour to the **Klamath Overlook** *(Requa Rd.)* for a lofty vantage point on the Klamath River entering the ocean. The seaward view here is so expansive you can discern the curvature of the earth, where water meets sky. When it's foggy, the bluffs slowly fade and trees blur, as in a Chinese watercolor.

A few miles north is the kitsch capital of redwood country, **Trees of Mystery** *(15500 US 101. 707-482-2251 or 800-638-3389. Adm. fee).* You can't miss the nearly 50-foot Paul Bunyan and his 35-foot blue ox companion out front, ballyhooing the commercial attractions—trees growing in unusual groupings, redwoods chain-saw-carved into cute storybook characters, and a vast gift shop. The **End of the**

Regeneration, Redwood National Park

Trail Indian Museum has five rooms of worthwhile artifacts.

Hiking through silent groves of second-growth redwoods and along spectacularly scenic coastal bluffs is the main attraction at **Del Norte Coast Redwoods State Park** *(US 101. 707-464-6101. Use fee).* The edge where two natural elements, earth and water, meet has its own drama. Beyond the park at **Enderts Beach** *(Enderts Beach Rd. off US 101),* take the

13

time to watch the surf surge against the rocks, bend over a tide pool to see a hermit crab walk around in someone else's shell, or observe a green anemone so plantlike it's hard to believe it's an animal.

At Crescent City, take US 199 east to **Jedediah Smith Redwoods State Park** *(707-464-6101. Use fee)*, named for a mountain man who in 1828 led a party through here on a bedeviled trek to the Pacific. Alongside the road flows the middle fork of a river that carries his name. It, like Smith, is a survivor—the last undammed river system in California. An angler's dream, where steelhead can weigh 20 pounds, the **Smith River** also plays host to frolicking otters and kayakers on its riffles and mild rapids.

Stay alongside the river on US 199 past the village of Gasquet, where you say good-bye to the fog and redwoods and enter a country of incense cedars and madrone. Along the river ahead look for jade-colored pools and waterfalls. To continue this California drive toward Yreka, you must enter Oregon, skirting the Siskiyou Mountains, which don't take kindly to roads. Head north on US 199 to O'Brien, Oregon, and turn right on Waldo Road to **Happy Camp Road** *(Also known as Indian Creek Rd. Closed in winter)*. (If it's winter, or if you don't care to negotiate a paved but winding mountain road, stay on US 199 north to Grants Pass, Oregon, then return south on I-5 to Yreka.) Happy Camp Road winds up to a summit of 4,812 feet and offers a spectacular view of the Indian Creek drainage. You'll follow Indian Creek through one of the only areas in California where rare Brewer's spruces grow.

After 38 miles you reach ❸ **Happy Camp,** a town that has suffered busts in both mining and timber. Today the bonanza is white-water rafting *(May-Oct.)* and some autumn fishing for salmon and steelhead. This is also a trailhead for the **Marble Mountain** and **Siskiyou Wilderness Areas** *(530-493-2243)*. From here eastward, Calif. 96 traces the **Klamath River** as it slides across meadows and plunges through chasms. To the south lie the Klamath Mountains, an extension of the Sierra Nevada made mostly of metamorphic rock.

Continue through **Seiad Valley,** wide open and dotted with farms. From the hamlet of **Horse Creek** you can poke

14

US 101 in Redwood National Park

up a narrow valley into ranch country. Continue on Calif. 96, passing through mixed conifers (pines, firs) and hardwoods (oak, madrone), as well as gorgeous gorges cut by the river.

To reach ❹ **Yreka** *(Chamber of Commerce, 117 W. Miner*

South Fork Smith River

St. 530-842-1649), turn south on either Calif. 263 or the faster but duller I-5. Born of an 1851 gold rush, Yreka preserves many historic commercial buildings, homes, and churches *(walking guide brochure available at chamber).* Downtown, gold nuggets are displayed at the 1850s **Siskiyou County Courthouse** *(311 4th St. Mon.-Fri.).* The indoor-outdoor **Siskiyou County Museum** *(910 S. Main St. 530-842-3836. Tues.-Sat.; adm. fee)* has

Yreka storefronts

exhibits on mining, fur trapping, and fossils, along with relics from Native American, pioneer, and military inhabitants. Also in the central part of town, the **Yreka Western Railroad** *(300 E. Miner St. 530-842-4146 or 800-973-5277. Mid-June–Labor Day Wed.-Sun., Labor Day–Oct. Sat.-Sun.; adm. fee)* runs the *Blue Goose,* a 1915 Baldwin steam locomotive pulling historic passenger cars on a three-hour jaunt through the Shasta Valley to the old railroad town of Montague.

South of Yreka, follow scenic **Calif. 3**★ into the Scott River Valley, where you'll have cattle for company. In **Fort Jones,** see the Indian baskets at the **Fort Jones Museum** *(530-468-5568. Mem. Day–Labor Day Mon.-Fri.),* and check out the Rain Rock, a two-ton boulder into which Klamath Indians pounded holes to bring rain. If too much rain came, they'd cover the holes to politely tell the Great Spirit that that was enough.

For pure inspiration, follow your feet into the **Marble Mountain Wilderness** ★ *(Klamath N.F. 530-842-6131),*

Camping in Trinity Alps Wilderness

16

whose high point is 8,299-foot Boulder Peak. Trails ascend from forests of mixed conifers up to alpine meadows, bare peaks, and lakes where you can camp and fish for trout.

The road passes through **Callahan,** with its 19th-century buildings. At Scott Mountain Summit (5,401 feet) it intersects the **Pacific Crest National Scenic Trail,** running north to Canada and south to Mexico (take your pick). You'll have the Trinity River beside you on the descent to **Coffee Creek,** an old gold-mining town.

Calif. 3 then rolls alongside **Clair Engle (Trinity) Lake,** popular with houseboaters, water-skiers, and fishermen. To the west rises the **Trinity Alps Wilderness** ★ *(530-623-2121. Wilderness permit required),* where you can explore 517,500 roadless acres of peaks, meadows, forests, streams, and lakes. Activities include backpacking, fishing, and hiking. A handy gateway is along the Stuart Fork *(Trinity Alps Rd.).*

Inhale the scent of ponderosa pines and Douglas-firs on the way into the gold rush town of ❺ **Weaverville** ★ *(Chamber of Commerce 530-623-6101).* At the **J.J. (Jake) Jackson Memorial Museum/Trinity County Historical Park** *(408 Main St. 530-623-5211. Daily April-Nov., Tues. and Sat. Dec.-March; donation),* the motto seems to be "a little

bit of everything." There are Victorian clothes, a steam-driven stamp mill, and even graffiti-scrawled jail cells. The museum also offers walking tour maps to the town's more than one hundred historic buildings, many on Main Street. If you need an aspirin or toothbrush, try the Weaverville Drug Store, California's oldest pharmacy, which has been dispensing such necessities since 1854.

Weaverville's Chinese community settled here during gold rush times and has never stopped worshiping at the town's 1874 Taoist temple, now part of **Weaverville Joss House State Historic Park** *(Oregon and Main Sts. 530-623-5284. Daily Mem. Day–Labor Day, Wed.-Sun. April–Mem. Day and Labor Day–Nov., Sat. only Dec.-March; adm. fee).* The gilded altars, figures of deities, and "spirit-summoning drum" may transport you to another world and another time.

To return to the ocean, drive Calif. 3 south through tiny towns such as Hayfork and Peanut before taking Calif. 36 west. At small **6** **Grizzly Creek Redwoods State Park** *(707-777-3683. Adm. fee)* you can pitch your tent where Native Americans once set up seasonal fishing camps during salmon and steelhead runs. Hike among redwoods and swim in the Van Duzen River. Though there are black bears in the area, no California grizzly bears live here anymore.

After you hit US 101 north, detour to the 1852 village of **Ferndale ★** *(Calif. 211. Chamber of Commerce 707-786-4477).* Resembling a Victorian storybook illustration, Ferndale is a montage of painted gingerbread houses *(walking tour guide available at Main St. shops).* Built by rich dairymen, these "butterfat palaces" reach a peak of whipped cream froth at the 1899 **Gingerbread Mansion** *(400 Berding St. Private).* The **Ferndale Museum** *(Shaw and 3rd Sts. 707-786-4466. June-Sept. Tues.-Sun., Oct.-May Wed.-Sun., closed Jan.; adm. fee)* traces the local blacksmithing, dairy, and logging industries. The **Kinetic Sculpture Race Museum** *(Shaw and Main Sts.)* displays people-powered vehicles used in an annual race from Arcata to Ferndale. More artistic than speedy, they include an enchanted slipper on wheels and something called the "Nightmare of the

Ferndale's Victoriana

Iguana." Also in town is **Russ Park,** a bird sanctuary with 110 acres of closed-canopy forest, laced with hiking trails. Return north to Eureka on US 101.

Lost Coast

Want to disappear for a while? Take a 65-mile detour along the "Lost Coast." After leaving Ferndale on Mattole Road, you climb among maples and evergreens, then through grassy hills. The road descends to ranch country where cows stare into space. Finally, you reach the ocean and wild **Cape Mendocino,** among the westernmost points in the contiguous 48 states. The road rolls south along a rocky shore with the look of perpetual low tide; the tidal zone rose 4 feet during a 1992 earthquake. At **Petrolia,** stop by the friendly store, then go on to **Honey Dew,** just a country store with a post office. Soon you enter the redwoods, leaving the Lost Coast for others to find.

17

The Cascades ★

● **260 miles** ● **2 to 3 days** ● **Spring through fall**
● **Lassen Park Road closed by snow in winter.**

A great presence makes itself felt in the southern Cascade Range, revered by Native Americans as a place of immense spiritual power. California writer Joaquin Miller called it "lonely as God and white as a winter moon." It is Mount Shasta, a dormant (but not extinct) volcano that rises to 14,162 feet and dominates the view for hundreds of miles around. This drive heads toward the mountain from historic Red Bluff, visiting Shasta Lake and the granite fortresses of Castle Crags State Park. Then it comes to Mount Shasta city, a mecca for climbers and skiers. The route swings east, stopping at a waterfall marveled at by Teddy Roosevelt, and winds south through Lassen Volcanic National Park, a haunting region of steam vents and bubbling mud pots that has been active for more than 600,000 years.

1 Red Bluff *(Chamber of Commerce 530-527-6220)* got its name from the steep red banks on a nearby curve of the Sacramento River. By 1850, steamers from San Francisco were plying the river to the town, the head of navigation. Historic buildings still stand on Main Street. An 1880s sheepman built the **Kelly-Griggs House Museum** *(311 Washington St. 530-527-1129. Thurs.-Sun.)*, which has antique furnishings and Victorian mannequins.

Drive 2 miles northeast to the **William B. Ide Adobe State Historic Park** *(21659 Adobe Rd. 530-529-8599. Parking fee)*. An 1850s house stands as a monument to the Massachusetts carpenter who led a mouse-that-roared rebellion against Mexican authorities in 1846. Remarkably, the rebels succeeded, installing Ide as president of the Bear Flag Republic—which fizzled a month later. The adobe house rests beside the Sacramento River in the shade of a huge valley oak. The park also includes a smokehouse and a carriage shed.

Follow I-5 through the northern Sacramento Valley, as it becomes more rolling and covered with trees. To the west rise the Trinity Mountains, to the east the Cascade Range—good company, indeed.

Continue to urban Redding and turn west on Calif. 299, going 6 miles to **2 Shasta State Historic Park** *(530-243-8194. Wed.-Sun.; adm. fee)*. In the forsaken streets of this 1850s gold rush camp, imagine whooping miners and clattering freight wagons. The ruins of Shasta City are of brick with iron shutters— sensible materials used after an 1853 fire nearly leveled the town, a commercial hub for surrounding mines. Explore the general store; cemetery; and courthouse museum, which holds gold rush relics such as guns and paintings, a restored court-

Fly-fishing on the Sacramento River, near Dunsmuir

room, and a sobering jail and double gallows.

As the terrain along I-5 turns more mountainous, take a side trip to **Shasta Dam★** *(6 miles W via Calif. 151. 530-275-4463. Tours available)*. Completed in 1945, the dam marks the beginning of California's massive Central Valley Project, which controls river flooding and impounds irrigation water for agriculture in the San Joaquin and Sacramento Valleys. Tours visit the spillway (nearly three times higher than Canada's Niagara Falls) and power plant, and visitors see devices that measure how much the dam moves and leaks. Also on view are exhibits concerning the new 64 million dollar temperature control device that draws water from different depths of the lake to maintain the correct downstream river temperature for spawning salmon. In the amazing statistics department: This hydroelectric dam produces enough power to light a city the size of San Francisco, and at 602 feet high and 3,460 feet long, it contains enough concrete to pave a sidewalk 3 feet wide and 4 inches deep all the way around the globe.

Paddling the Sacramento River

The dam holds back the waters of the Sacramento, McCloud, and Pit Rivers, creating **Shasta Lake** ★ *(530-275-5555 or 800-326-6944)*. When full, the lake's five arms constitute the state's largest reservoir, with 370 miles of shoreline (more than San Francisco Bay). Anglers go after bass, trout, and salmon, while vacationers go water-skiing, canoeing, and parasailing. Also consider the vast flotilla of houseboats for rent, offering a leisurely way to explore the lake for a few days

1850s gold rush camp, now Shasta State Historic Park

(although you won't necessarily be alone, as this recreational hot spot attracts three million visitors a year).

Is it hot today? For a sanctuary that's always 58°F, hop a ferry across the lake to **Lake Shasta Caverns** *(O'Brien–Shasta Caverns Rd. exit off I-5, then ferry across lake. 530-238-2341 or 800-795-2283. Adm. fee)*. In underground chambers you'll see "waterfalls" of milky white flowstone and fluted columns and stone draperies 120 feet high, all created by water seeping through limestone. Look for the name of the cave's discoverer on the wall, written in 1878 with carbide from his miner's lamp.

Keep going north on I-5 through forested mountains. Ahead rise the gray pinnacles of ❸ **Castle Crags State Park** ★ *(Castella exit. 530-235-2684. Adm. fee)*, formed of granitic material slowly forced up through the surrounding serpentine rock and later polished by glaciers. The heights are forested with evergreens; the lower elevations add oaks and bigleaf maples that turn colors in autumn. Two miles of the Sacramento River run through the park, as do 9 miles of the Pacific Crest National Scenic Trail. **Vista Point** has a nice prospect of Mount Shasta and the crags. In this rough country, settlers and Modoc Indians fought a fierce battle in 1855.

Located beside its namesake mountain, the town of **Mount Shasta** *(Visitors Bureau 530-926-4865 or 800-926-4865)* has become a headquarters not only for skiers and hikers, but also for nontraditional religions and New Age groups. Some regard the volcano as a "cosmic vortex," where it's possible to commune with spiritual beings, while other believers say it's the home of Lemurians (from Mu, the Pacific Ocean's Atlantis), Bigfoot, or space beings who materialize at will.

Castle Crags State Park

21

A magical place right in town is **Big Springs** *(City Park, off N. Mt. Shasta Blvd.)*, the northernmost feeder stream of the Sacramento River. Watch as clear, icy water flows from a lava tube originating deep within Mount Shasta. Presto! Instant river. This marvel takes place in a wooded public park.

Just outside town, at the 1888 **Mount Shasta Hatchery** *(3 N. Old Stage Rd. 530-926-2215)*, you'll see fish in all stages of growth and get the chance to feed them. In early days, biologists here stocked mountain lakes by carrying trout in packs on muleback. Today fingerlings are dropped into the water from an airplane! The nearby **Sisson Museum** *(530-926-5508. April-Dec.)* has displays on local history and ecology, and (for some reason) a 9-foot-tall teddy bear.

Before taking a summer hike on **Mount Shasta** ★ ★,

be sure to stop at the local ranger station *(204 W. Alma. 530-926-4511)* for trail conditions and wilderness regulations. The most popular trail leads to Horse Camp, a stone cabin built by the Sierra Club in 1922; it starts at Bunny Flat, located 11 miles up Everitt Memorial High-

Mount Shasta peaks

Climbers' camp, Mount Shasta

way, the only paved road to timberline. The road ends at 7,800 feet at the Ski Bowl, where you have a chest-swelling view of Mount Lassen, Castle Crags, Mount Eddy, and the Trinity Alps. Climbing to the summit *(best from June-Sept. Wilderness permit required; check climbing conditions)*, a strenuous ascent to 14,162 feet that requires crampons and an ice axe, is within reach of most physically fit people.

Head east on Calif. 89 and take the turnoff for **Mount Shasta Ski Park** *(Ski Park Hwy. 530-926-8686)*, where "ski" means both downhill and cross-country. In summer, take a scenic chairlift ride, or strap your mountain bike next to you and then bomb down the slopes courtesy of gravity.

Continue to **McCloud** *(Chamber of Commerce 530-964-2604)*, a lumber mill's "company town" from 1897 to 1962;

the historic area is lined with uniformly styled wooden buildings. The **Heritage Junction Museum of McCloud** *(520 Main St. 530-964-2604. May-Oct.)* commemorates the short line railroad that hauled logs to the mill and displays the beloved steam engine that ran mill operations.

Mount Shasta: Fire and Ice

To the Wintu Indians, the great volcano standing alone—a white mass rising 10,000 feet above the surrounding land—was directly connected to the spirit world. Certainly it is a godly realm, a place of elemental fire and ice. Near the summit hot springs steam—evidence of volcanic heat deep below; and yet five glaciers survive in a perennial deep freeze. Mount Shasta has blown its stack about ten times in the past 4,500 years. The latest eruption, apparently in 1786, deposited a mantle of brown pumice that's easy to discern. Will Shasta erupt again? Yes. But scientists believe the volcano will show warning signs first: small earthquakes, gas emissions, swelling flanks, and more activity in local thermal springs.

Keep driving 5 miles east to **McCloud River Falls** *(530-964-2184),* which has three gorgeous cascades spilling into deep pools. The lower falls are accessible by car, and, if icy water is no deterrent, you can swim.

A couple miles ahead on Calif. 89, there's a viewpoint where the white mass of Mount Shasta seems almost to levitate above the trees. After Dead Horse Summit (4,533 feet) the road eases down through deep pines. Don't miss ❹ **McArthur-Burney Falls Memorial State Park** ★ *(24898 Calif. 89. 530-335-2777. Adm. fee),* aptly labeled "a wonder" by Teddy Roosevelt. Here twin cascades tumble 129 feet into an emerald pool, raising mists that sunshine often suffuses with rainbow light. Equally marvelous, an underground stream emerges through crevices in the mossy basalt wall, releasing ribbons of water. There's also a lake where you might see great blue herons or bald eagles.

Drive south through horse ranching country along Hat Creek, prime water for trout fishing. Ahead you'll pass lava flows interspersed with forested creeks and pastures.

Stop at **Subway Cave,** a 2,000-year-old lava tube that you can walk into for a quarter mile; the tunnel is cold and dark, so bring a jacket and at least two flashlights. At Old Station, Calif. 89 melds with Calif. 44 west. A

McArthur-Burney Falls Memorial State Park

24

couple of miles ahead stop at the **vista point** and look south to where the region's lava came from, Lassen Peak.

Follow Calif. 89 into 106,000-acre ❺ **Lassen Volcanic National Park** ★ ★ *(530-595-4444. Adm. fee. Road closed in winter),* one of the few places in the world that brings you every type of volcano: shield, plug dome, composite, and cinder cone. The park is also a living laboratory of hydrothermal features—steam vents (fumaroles), mud pots, boiling pools—every type but geysers. Conifer forests soften the craters and lava rubble. The park drive winds around the Cascades' southernmost volcano, Lassen Peak (10,457 feet). At the height of its last eruption cycle in 1915, Lassen blew a black mushroom cloud of ash, steam, and rocks about 6 miles into the sky.

Just inside the park, stop for a lesson in volcanology at the **Loomis Museum** *(530-595-4444 ext. 5180. Daily July-Sept., Sat.-Sun. Mem. Day–June).* Picnic at adjacent **Manzanita Lake,** created by a massive rockfall across a creek and home to ducks and geese. Ahead and to the south you'll see tall formations called the **Chaos Crags** *(Milepost 63).* Three centuries ago swarms of boulders tumbled down from those heights. They are now known as the **Chaos Jumbles** *(Mile 62).*

At Nobles Pass *(Mile 60)* you meet the **Nobles Emigrant Trail,** used in the 1850s by travelers crossing the continent. Ahead, the **Devastated Area** *(Miles 44, 41)* shows the path of a mudflow from Lassen's 1915 blowup, which also flattened trees in a mile-wide swath.

Park the car and hike the 2.5 miles to the 10,457-foot summit of **Lassen Peak** *(Mile 22)*. On the bare, stony slope there is neither shade nor water, so prepare accordingly. At **Bumpass Hell** *(Mile 17)* a trail leads among bubbling pools, gas vents, and gurgling mud pots. But don't get off the boardwalk; the area is named for a mid-19th-century guide named Bumpass, whose leg plunged through the flimsy rock crust into a thermal pool; his parboiled limb had to be amputated.

For an easier walk try the **Sulphur Works** *(Mile 5)*, identifiable by the rotten-egg smell emitted from the steam vents and mud pots. These mark the main vent system of a giant ancient volcano called Mount Tehama, which once towered 11,500 feet; it eroded away, leaving only a few remnants such as nearby **Brokeoff Mountain.** Just ahead, the Southwest Entrance Station has information on the park.

Lassen Peak looming over remains of Mount Tehama

Take Calif. 89 south to Calif. 36 west, and descend to the small town of **Mineral,** set among pines and firs. About 8 miles ahead you leave the forest and enter oak woodlands. Before Paynes Creek is an overlook into stream-carved Battle Creek Canyon. Continue to Red Bluff, the drive's end.

North Coast ★

● 260 miles ● 2 to 3 days ● Year-round ● Avoid driving south on Calif. 1 in heavy fog or darkness.

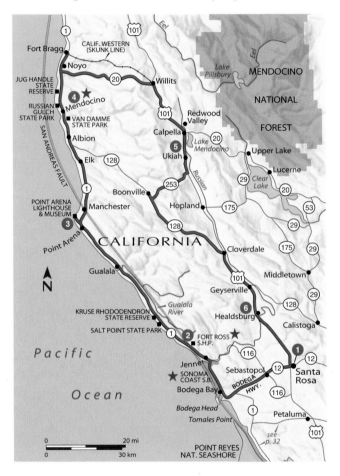

From busy Santa Rosa, this drive leads west to a wild stretch of the Pacific coast, following the ragged edge of the continent northward. Highlights include the mouth of the Russian River, state parks, a historic Russian fort, and the New England-style village of Mendocino (which might look familiar as Cabot Cove of television's *Murder, She Wrote*). The route next turns inland, visiting a town that created its own language, then uncorks itself in friendly wine country.

Amid the modern sprawl of ❶ **Santa Rosa** *(Visitors Bureau 707-577-8674)* you'll discover the legacies of two intriguing men. Horticulturist Luther Burbank developed more than 800 new varieties of plants, including the Shasta daisy. After moving to town in 1875, the plant wizard worked for 53 years at the **Luther Burbank Home & Gardens** ★ *(Santa Rosa and Sonoma Aves. 707-524-5445. Gardens daily; house and greenhouse tour April-Oct. Wed.-Sun.; fee for tour).* See the carriage house museum and Burbank's home, where Thomas Edison and Helen Keller came to call.

Where else can you see a "fur-bearing trout" except at the **Church of One Tree/Robert L . "Believe It Or Not!"®** **Ripley Memorial Museum** *(492 Sonoma Ave. 707-524-5233. April-Oct. Wed.-Sun.; adm. fee),* across Santa Rosa Avenue. The unusual memorabilia of the local cartoonist who created "Believe It Or Not!"® are displayed in a church made from a single redwood. An oddity himself, Ripley used to work in his bathrobe with chipmunks running around on his desk.

Take Calif. 12 west to **Sebastopol** *(Chamber of Commerce 707-823-3032),* where apple trees grow heavy with Gravensteins around the late July to September harvesttime. Local orchards sell apples, as well as jam and cider.

Follow Bodega Highway to Calif. 1 and the fishing village of **Bodega Bay** *(Chamber of Commerce 707-875-3422).* Eerily familiar? Yes, if you saw Alfred Hitchcock's spooky movie *The Birds,* which was filmed here. Drive out to **Bodega Head** for big views of the coast.

Heading north on Calif. 1, you pass headlands and sandy strands brought together as the **Sonoma Coast State Beach** ★ *(707-875-3483),* sublime for tide pooling and sunbathing. View the offshore sea stacks and crashing surf, but treacherous currents forbid swimming.

Luther Burbank Home & Gardens, Santa Rosa

Where the Russian River slips into the ocean stands the tiny settlement of **Jenner.** At **Goat Rock Beach,** harbor seals raise their pups *(March-April).* Look for ospreys fishing in the estuary.

Soon the road climbs to nearly a thousand feet above the ocean, offering dramatic views. Through the woods ahead you'll see the palisades and Russian Orthodox chapel of ❷ **Fort Ross State Historic Park** ★ *(707-847-3286. Adm.*

fee), where Russians came in 1812 to collect sea otter pelts and raise food for their Alaska settlers. At Fort Ross (short for Rossiya) you'll see reconstructed blockhouses and living quarters. The sole original structure is the circa 1836 residence of Manager Rotchev, a poet who married a princess. After the Russians nearly wiped out the otter population, they abandoned the fort in 1841.

Farther north, **Salt Point State Park** *(25050 Calif. 1. 707-847-3221. Adm. fee)* has two faces. One looks toward the sea, with easy-to-reach tide pools, a harbor seal colony, a coastal hiking trail, and an underwater preserve at Gerstle Cove. The park's other face turns toward the hills, where tan oaks and redwoods grow, and trails lead to a pygmy tree forest. Along the park's north edge is **Kruse Rhododendron State Reserve,** where Douglas-firs and redwoods create a green backdrop for pink rhododendrons that burst into bloom in late April and May. Hiking trails wind through fern-filled canyons.

28

Chapel, Fort Ross State Historic Park

The Gualala River enters the ocean at the old lumber town of **Gualala** (wa-LA-la), whose 1903 hotel is the hub of local social life. Ahead in microscopic **Point Arena,** fishermen in rubber boots tromp alongside hippies in tie-dyed clothes on the historic Main Street. Tide poolers and surfers enjoy **Arena Cove,** which also has a fishing pier.

A few miles north is the turnoff to **❸ Point Arena Lighthouse and Museum** *(707-882-2777. Adm. fee. Overnight accommodations available).* Climb the 115-foot tower of this 1907 lighthouse for a stunning view of the coastline and of migrating gray whales *(Dec.-April).* See the crystal-and-brass Fresnel lens that weighs two tons and the displays about shipwrecks.

In the tide pools at **Van Damme State Park** *(707-937-5804. Adm. fee),* 2 miles south of Mendocino, you can observe the housing arrangements of sea stars, anemones, sea urchins, and crabs. Walk through a fern-laced river canyon or visit a forest of stunted pines and cypresses.

Settled in 1852, the coastal village of **❹ Mendocino**★ *(Chamber of Commerce 707-961-6300 or 800-726-2780)* blends the traditional style of New England saltbox and Victorian houses with the anarchic spirit of an alternative community of the sixties. The former lumber town has been an artists' colony since the late 1950s, when a local man opened a coin laundry with an art gallery upstairs. The **Mendocino**

Art Center *(45200 Little Lake St. 707-937-5818 or 800-653-3328)* shows mostly local paintings, weavings, ceramics, and photography. Visitors browse in fine art galleries, as well as

Coastline along Calif. 1, near Jenner

shops with tourist-oriented arts and crafts.

At the 1854 **Ford House Visitor Center and Museum** *(735 Main St. 707-937-5397. Donation),* you'll see a scale model of the town in 1890, complete with water towers, cemetery, and the lumber chutes that occupied the headlands. The nearby **Kelley House Museum** *(45007 Albion St. 707-937-4791. Daily May-Sept., Fri.-Mon. Oct.-April)* displays local history artifacts, and the 1882 **MacCallum House Restaurant and Inn** *(45020 Albion St. 707-937-0289)* has a pleasant cottage garden.

Wrapping around three sides of town, **Mendocino Headlands State Park** *(707-937-5397)* preserves sandstone bluffs, wave tunnels, tide pools, beaches, and grasslands, and offers views big enough to expand anyone's horizons. In winter, this is prime whale-watching territory. A self-guided tour map of the headlands is available at the Ford House.

Along Calif. 1 outside Mendocino

On the way farther north, stop to hike amid redwood forests, ferns, and wild ginger to reach the waterfall at **Russian Gulch State Park** *(707-937-5804. Adm. fee)*. Farther along, explore a series of stair-stepped marine terraces at **Jug Handle State Reserve** *(707-937-5804)*; each level supports a different group of plants and trees. Then stop at the harbor town of **Noyo** for seafood—salmon, crab, albacore—fresh from the boat.

Fort Bragg *(Chamber of Commerce 707-961-6300 or 800-726-2780)* began in the 1850s as a military post, then grew into a lumbering center. The **Guest House Museum** *(343 N. Main St. 707-961-2840. Closed Mon.)* has exhibits on town history and early lumbering. The town's main attraction is a ride on the **Skunk Line** *(707-964-6371. Fare)*, which leaves the circa 1924 railroad depot and snakes through mountains and redwoods to Willits. The train was named for its original gas engines—you smelled them before you could see them.

Backtrack south to Calif. 20, a forested route heading east to **Willits.** Pause for a peek at the redwood train station *(E. Commercial St.)*, variously described as "dowdy" and "frumpy." Heading south now on US 101, you cross Ridgewood Summit, once the haunt of Black Bart, a notorious gentleman bandit of the 1880s who held up stagecoaches and left behind scraps of poetry. (See sidebar p. 100).

⑤ Ukiah *(Chamber of Commerce 707-462-4705)* means "deep valley" in the language of the Pomo Indians, whose culture is celebrated at the **Grace Hudson Museum and the Sun House** *(431 S. Main St. 707-467-2836. Wed.-Sun.; donation)*. Among the changing displays are Hudson's turn-of-the-century portraits of Pomo people, along with Indian baskets collected by her ethnologist husband. In 1911, the bohemian couple built Sun House, a craftsman-style bungalow; their eclectic belongings include a melodeon and Limoges china.

Riding the Skunk Line from Fort Bragg

From Ukiah, head west on Calif. 253 to Calif. 128 and the rustic town of **Boonville** *(Chamber of Commerce 707-895-2379)*. While here, why not have a "horn of zeese"? Or use the "buckey walter"? This lingo is Boontling, the town's unique home-grown language (see sidebar p. 30).

Boonville serves as a gateway to the **Anderson Valley** ★, a region of vineyards and apple orchards. About a

Coastal fog in Mendocino County

mile north of town, a red schoolhouse, sheep shearing shed, and other buildings house the **Anderson Valley Historical Museum** *(Calif. 128 at Anderson Valley Way. Open when flags are flying)*, with exhibits on home life, farming, and Boontling.

Wind southeast on Calif. 128 through hills dotted with weathered barns and oak trees, then turn south at Cloverdale on US 101. You'll see vineyards on the way into the 1850s town of ❻ **Healdsburg** *(Visitors Bureau, 217 Healdsburg Ave. 707-433-6935)*; it's the crossroads of the **Russian River, Dry Creek**, and **Alexander Valleys** ★, which are home to more than 50 wineries *(map and guide brochure available at Visitors Bureau)*. Compared to upscale Napa Valley, the area has a small-town atmosphere. A 1910 Carnegie library now houses the **Healdsburg Museum** *(221 Matheson St. 707-431-3325. Closed Mon.)*, with its Pomo and Wappo baskets and historical oddities such as a porcelain Chinese bowl that was carried across the country seven times by covered wagon, and survived intact.

Finish this drive by returning south to Santa Rosa.

Napa Valley and

● 185 miles ● 2 to 3 days ● Year-round ● On weekends in summer and during autumn grape crushing, Calif. 29 in Napa Valley can be as crowded as Disneyland's parking lot. In that case, drive the quieter Silverado Trail that parallels the highway to the east.

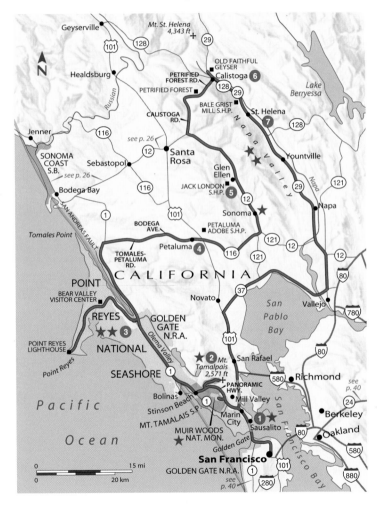

Ahead of you lie many wonders of northern California—redwood forests, remote seashores, rural towns, and the wine country of the famous Sonoma and Napa Valleys—all within a reasonable drive from San Francisco (see p. 40).

Beginning in San Francisco, cross the **Golden Gate Bridge**★★ on US 101 north. On the other side, take a quick detour to a 360-degree, bird's-eye vantage of the bridge from Marin Headlands *(Alexander Ave. exit, take an immediate left, following signs back to San Francisco. At the sign for Marin Headlands turn right, go uphill 0.3 mile and park).*

Back on US 101, you soon reach a tunnel that seems to promise good things: Over the entrance, someone has painted a bright rainbow. This is the gateway to **Marin County,** the upscale residential area where the eighties' Me Generation poured itself a glass of white wine and soaked communally in a redwood hot tub.

Off US 101 just ahead, houses clinging to wooded hillsides above a yacht harbor give ➊ **Sausalito ★** *(Visitor Center 415-332-0505)* the look of a European seacoast resort. Shop in turn-of-the-century buildings along Bridgeway; dine; or sample saloons where locals mix with tourists, boat

Golden Gate Bridge in afternoon fog

33

buffs, aging coquettes, bikers, and bohemians. Along the waterfront look for houseboats *(Gate 5 and other locations).* See the **San Francisco Bay Model and Visitors Center** *(Marinship Way. 415-332-3871. Call for schedule),* a huge working rendition of San Francisco Bay and its tides that condenses about 400 square miles to 1.5 acres.

Continue on US 101, exiting onto Calif. 1 just north of Marin City. In about 3 miles turn right onto Panoramic Highway, then left on Muir Woods Road. You're heading for the area's last virgin redwood forest, **Muir Woods National Monument ★** *(415-388-2595).* Thousand-year-old trees soaring as high as 254 feet create a cathedral atmosphere, interrupted only by the squawk of Steller's jays. Redwood Creek shelters crayfish, salmon, and steelhead trout. Six different trails, including one with interpretive signs, wander through this majestic sanctuary.

For the big picture, continue on Panoramic Highway, turn right on Pan Toll Road (follow sign), and ascend the east peak of ❷ **Mount Tamalpais** ★ *(Mt. Tamalpais S.P. 415-388-2070. Parking fee),* where locals claim to have invented mountain biking. Along Mount Tam's 200-plus miles of trails grow bouquets of spring wildflowers, including star lily, columbine, and Indian paintbrush. From the parking lot a quarter-mile path climbs to a fire lookout at the 2,571-foot summit, with its inspiring panorama of the bay area and the Pacific Ocean. This place seems somehow closer to the sun.

Sunning at Stinson Beach

Farther ahead, Panoramic Highway winds downhill among grassy slopes and stands of redwood, bay, and eucalyptus trees to **Stinson Beach,** popular for swimming and surfing. The village itself is a blink-and-you-missed-it place.

Heading north on Calif. 1, look for egrets and waterfowl as you pass **Bolinas Lagoon;** on two island sanctuaries, harbor seals have set up colonies. Next pop into **Audubon Canyon Ranch** ★ *(415-868-9244. Mid-March–mid-July Sat.-Sun.),* where egrets and herons nest in a 1,000-acre reserve;

some 115 bird species have been spotted.

The route passes eucalyptus trees and cows on its straight run through the Olema Valley—just another name for the San Andreas Fault. Calif. 1 follows this monumental fracture in the earth's surface. The fault line is

Redwood trees at Muir Woods National Monument

also traced on an interpretive trail at the Bear Valley Visitor Center of ❸ **Point Reyes National Seashore** ★★ *(Bear Valley Rd. 415-663-1092)*, one of several trails that wind throughout the park. In one afternoon you can sample four life zones: forest (Douglas-firs, ferns, huckleberries), coastline (osprey feeding on fish), grasslands (hilltops and gullies), and coastal wetlands (marshes, lagoons). Life is rich: Nearly half the bird species in North America have been seen here, from hawks to tufted puffins, and if you were to scoop up a handful of mud from a salt marsh, you might find 20,000 worms and other organisms—if that's your idea of a good time. Because the peninsula juts into the Pacific, it's a good place to observe migrating gray whales *(late Dec.–mid-March)*; the best whale-watching spot is the picturesque **Point Reyes Lighthouse,** though the place can be windy and cold.

Follow Calif. 1 to the north end of Tomales Bay and turn inland on Tomales-Petaluma Road to ❹ **Petaluma** *(Chamber of Commerce 707-769-0429)*. This town looks timelessly all-American, which explains why such movies as *American Graffiti* were filmed here. Downtown by the Petaluma River stand beautifully restored commercial buildings with cast-iron facades; these Victorians date from the turn of the century, when the surrounding poultry region grew wealthy as the "world's egg basket." The **Petaluma Historical Museum and Library** *(20 4th St. 707-778-4398. Thurs.-Mon.)* displays local memorabilia in a 1906 Carnegie library that has California's largest freestanding stained-glass dome. On a hilltop at the edge of town, **Petaluma Adobe State Historic Park** *(3325 Adobe Rd. 707-762-4871. Adm. fee)* preserves California's biggest non-mission adobe structure, the two-story ranch

35

San Andreas Fault

The famous 1906 "San Francisco" earthquake occurred along the notorious San Andreas Fault, a boundary between two large plates of the earth's crust, which grind past each other at the rate of about two inches a year in some places. Friction along the plates can lock them together temporarily, until they rupture suddenly and the stored energy is released as an earthquake. The 1906 shaker measured 7.7 on the moment-magnitude scale, releasing almost 30 times more energy than the 1989 Loma Prieta quake.

Napa Valley and the Pacific

A Primer on Wine Tasting

Don't be intimidated when some smug wine buff calls a wine "nervy" or "muscular." Most wine terms are subjective. If *you* like a wine, that's all that matters. Simply use your senses:

Sight: Each wine variety has an ideal color. Chardonnay, for instance, should be rich gold; a pale straw color might mean it hasn't developed full complexity.

Smell: Swirling wine in your glass releases chemical compounds you can smell. "Aroma" is the smell of the grape. "Bouquet" is the aroma plus fragrances from the wine's development (yeast, oak from the aging barrel).

Taste: Our taste buds detect only sweet (front of tongue), sour (edges), salty (middle), and bitter (back). To taste fruitiness, draw a sip up the middle of your tongue. For acid (which gives life and balance), roll the wine around the edges.

Feel: Warm a sip in your mouth, then judge its "body" — how thick or thin it feels. A lush feel is sometimes described as "velvet."

house of Mexican general Mariano Vallejo. He began building this hacienda in 1836, mostly to fend off Russian fur traders. His quarters and workrooms are furnished to reflect California's Mexican period.

From Petaluma, drive east on Calif. 116 and 121, then head north on Calif. 12 to **Sonoma** ★ *(Visitors Bureau 707-996-1090)*, a town where history comes alive. In the plaza in 1846, rebellious American settlers and trappers took Vallejo prisoner during the short-lived Bear Flag Revolt, in which they declared California an independent republic. On the plaza lies **Sonoma State Historic Park** ★ *(Spain St. between 2nd St. E. and 3rd St. W. 707-938-1519. Adm. fee)*, encompassing Mission San Francisco Solano (1823), which includes the last and most northerly of the 21 California missions; a barracks that housed Mexican and later American soldiers (now a museum); the wood-frame Toscano Hotel; and the adobe Blue Wing Inn of 1840, whose saloon was visited by Kit Carson and notorious bandit Joaquin Murietta. Half a mile west of the plaza stands Vallejo's New England-style home, **Lachryma Montis** *(Spain St. W. and 3rd St. W.)*.

Sonoma, known as the birthplace of the California wine industry, was planted with Franciscan mission grapes in 1825; some of the original plot is incorporated into **Sebastiani Vineyards** *(389 4th St. E. 707-938-5532 or 800-888-5532)*, which displays a large collection of carved wine casks. Premium winemaking began in 1857 at what is now the **Buena Vista Carneros Winery** *(18000 Old Winery Rd. 707-938-1266)*, whose stone cellars are the oldest in the state.

You'll see grape arbors as you travel north through Sonoma Valley to ❺ **Jack London State Historic Park** *(2400 London Ranch Rd., Glen Ellen. 707-938-5216. Adm. fee)*, the 835-acre ranch of the popular author of *The Call of the Wild*. The House of Happy Walls, built by his widow in 1919, contains mementos, art objects collected in the South Pacific, and London's typewriter. (Remarkably, even the author of 53 books got publishers' rejection slips.) An earlier mansion called Wolf House burned mysteriously before the Londons moved in; its ruined walls and fireplaces are visible.

Ahead you'll wind through some backcountry, following Calif. 12 north to the outskirts of Santa Rosa. Turn right onto Calistoga Road; at the intersection with Petrified Forest Road, go right again. About 4 miles before Calistoga you reach the **Petrified Forest** *(4100 Petrified Forest Rd. 707-942-6667. Adm. fee)*, a preserve of redwoods

flattened by volcanic eruption some 3.4 million years ago
and turned to stone. One trunk measures 108 feet long.

Now you enter **Napa Valley** ★ ★ *(Visitors Bureau 707-226-
7459)*, a great cornucopia of wine grapes spilling southward

Sonoma Valley vineyard

from 4,343-foot Mount St. Helena. The valley has ideal
growing conditions, with a dry Mediterranean climate
and rich, porous soils. Part agricultural belt and part
trendy destination for wine buffs, Napa Valley produces many of California's great vintages. Along the
valley's main artery, Calif. 29, lie many wineries—
famous names like Charles Krug, Robert Mondavi,
Beaulieu, and Beringer. You can tour them and taste
premium varieties, notably Chardonnay, Cabernet
Sauvignon, and Pinot Noir. Equally satisfying is the
sight of spring mustard flowers on the valley floor;
the surrounding mountains of the Coast Ranges;
and the oaks, California bays, and blackberries that
grow along the Napa River.

There's always a hot time in the old town of
❻ **Calistoga** *(Chamber of Commerce 707-942-6333)*.
Its thermal springs have been drawing travelers
since 1859, when California's first millionaire, colorful Sam Brannan, opened a mineral spa for wealthy San
Franciscans. The story goes that he intended to promote

Wine tasting at
Hess Collection Winery

37

his enterprise as the "Saratoga of California," but at a banquet he imbibed a bit of the bubbly before his speech and the phrase came out "Calistoga of Sarafornia." It's easy to picture the resort through some remarkable dioramas, made by a Disney artist, at the **Sharpsteen Museum** *(1311 Washington St. 707-942-5911)*, which also has an original furnished cottage.

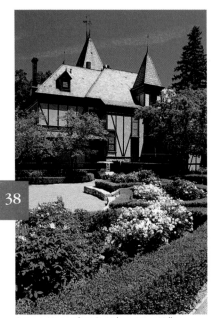

People still visit Calistoga spas to soak in hot mineral water or in vats of volcanic mud, said to be therapeutic. You have your choice of many spas around town, including **Calistoga Spa Hot Springs** *(1006 Washington St. 707-942-6269. Fee)*.

Only three geysers in the world erupt on a handy schedule—in Yellowstone National Park, in New Zealand, and near Calistoga. Just outside town, the **Old Faithful Geyser of California** *(1299 Tubbs Ln. 707-942-6463. Adm. fee)* shoots a blast of water 60 to 80 feet high every 40 minutes on average. The water is 350°F, and the sulfur smells like rotten eggs.

Beringer Vineyards in St. Helena, Napa Valley

Five miles south of Calistoga, stop by **Bale Grist Mill State Historic Park** *(707-942-4575. Adm. fee)*, which preserves the region's oldest water-powered grain mill (1847) in a pleasant wooded setting.

Onward to ❼ **St. Helena** *(Chamber of Commerce 707-963-4456 or 800-799-6456)*, an increasingly upscale town where you might see field-workers in muddy pickup trucks parked next to urbanites in BMWs.

The valley's oldest wine producer is St. Helena's **Charles Krug Winery** *(2800 Main St. 707-967-2201)*, founded in 1861. At the nearby 1876 **Beringer Vineyards** *(2000 Main St. 707-*

963-7115), tours visit tunnels a thousand feet long, dug by Chinese laborers and used to age wine. The vineyard's star attraction is the Rhine House, a 17-room Germanic mansion rich with carved wood and gemlike stained-glass windows.

The widely traveled Scottish author Robert Louis Stevenson spent his honeymoon in a mining shack on Mount St. Helena in 1880. Chronicling his life, the collection at the **Silverado Museum** *(1490 Library Ln. 707-963-3757. Closed Mon.; donation)* ranges from the toy soldiers of his boyhood to handwritten pages and first editions of *Treasure Island.*

Leaving St. Helena, you'll pass more wineries on the way south to Napa. Continue on Calif. 29 to Calif. 37, turning west along San Pablo Bay. Then go south on US 101.

You can get off in **Mill Valley,** a wooded enclave

Hot air balloon over Napa Valley

where self-development is a cottage industry. People seem to be constantly reinventing themselves as massage therapists, free-range chicken farmers, or channelers of guides from the spirit world—*very* Marin County. Continue to the Golden Gate, wrapping up the route in a neat loop.

San Francisco Bay Area ★

● 155 miles ● 2 to 3 days ● Year-round ● Avoid freeways during rush hour. Parking places are scarce in San Francisco; best to use public transportation.

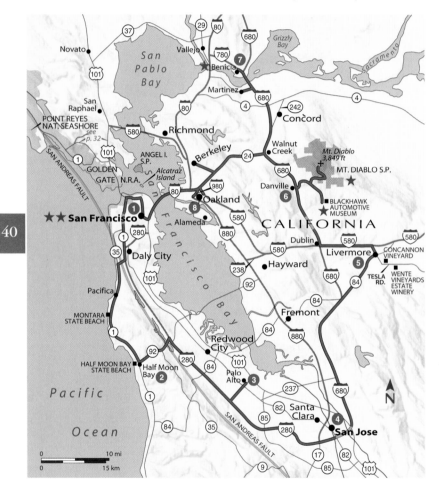

see p. 32

This loop drive begins in many travelers' favorite American city, San Francisco, which you'll explore from the top of Telegraph Hill to the bottom of the chowder bowls on Fisherman's Wharf. The city (never "Frisco") is situated on the tip of a peninsula, upon which the route leads south to burgeoning San Jose, the capital of Silicon Valley. Then you return north along the east side of San Francisco Bay, passing through small historic towns and the university city of Berkeley before arriving back in San Francisco.

Here's a city that has it all—heart-swelling views, a

picturesque bay that is by turns sunny or shrouded in romantic fog, Victorian houses on steep hills, fine restaurants, and high culture. **1** **San Francisco**★★ *(Visitor Information Center 415-391-2000)* started out as a rough-and-tumble child of the California Gold Rush. With its new wealth, the town picked up big-city sophistication and style, but always kept its bohemian soul. Its reputation for tolerance made San Francisco a home of the 1950s beat generation and the hippie-go-lucky generation of the sixties; today it's a capital of the gay community.

The heart of downtown is **Union Square,** a plaza planted with boxwoods and bright flowers. Scores of elegant hotels, clothiers, and restaurants surround it.

Before exploring northward on your tour of the city, duck south of Market Street to the **San Francisco Museum of Modern Art**★ *(151 3rd St. 415-357-4000. Closed Wed.; adm. fee).* With appropriately modernist lines, the West Coast MoMA houses more than 17,000 modern works, specializing in Mexican painting, fauvism, German expressionism, and American abstract expressionism. Famous works range from Matisse's "Femme au Chapeau". (1907) to pop artist Andy Warhol's "National Velvet" (1963).

Transamerica building in downtown San Francisco

Also south of Market, in the Mission District, wisps of incense and the past permeate San Francisco's oldest building. Built in 1791 along California's chain of missions, **Mission San Francisco de Asís (Mission Dolores)** *(16th and Dolores Sts. 415-621-8203. Adm. fee)* still has its painted ceiling and original bells.

Back at Union Square, you're in a good place to board the city's unique **cable cars**★ *(415-673-6864. Fare),* clanking machine-age delights that "climb halfway to the stars." To see an original 1873 model and the powerhouse that drives the entire system, catch a ride from Powell Street to the **San Francisco Cable Car Museum** *(Washington and Mason Sts. 415-474-1887).*

Nearby **Chinatown**★ *(Grant Ave. area bet. Bush and Broad-*

Birds of Alcatraz

In a place where jailbirds once attempted to fly the coop—that is, the federal "pen" on Alcatraz Island —other kinds of birds are nesting nowadays. Naturalists have counted more than 1,000 pairs of western gulls (Feb.-Sept.), black-crowned night herons, and cormorants (both May-Aug.). This represents a real comeback. It's believed that Native Americans may have once collected eggs for food. Later, a military fort and prison buildings took up nesting areas. Today, visitors touring the penitentiary will see cormorants with their wings outstretched to dry after an underwater pursuit of fish. In June, tourists can approach within a few feet of gulls and their cute spotted chicks. Naturalists have banded many of the birds, which they recognize by their numbers. Hmmm . . . isn't that the same way Alcatraz prisoners used to be identified?

way) is a maze of sights and smells—pagoda roofs and dragon-entwined lampposts, restaurants, and shops crammed to the rafters with Asian arts both fine and facsimile. To learn about the Chinese who came to San Francisco during the gold rush visit the **Chinese Historical Society of America** (*650 Commercial St. 415-391-1188. Call for hours*). For architecture, see the painted balconies and temples along Waverly Place. Stockton Street is the neighborhood market, offering ginger roots and bamboo shoots and crates of cackling chickens.

That aroma—is it espresso? Follow your nose northward along Columbus Avenue into **North Beach,** whose coffeehouses were haunts of the beat generation in the fifties. Must-sees include **Washington Square,** the social hub of Little Italy, edged by beautiful **Saints Peter and Paul Church;** and **City Lights Booksellers** (*261 Columbus Ave. 415-362-8193*), founded in 1953 by beat poet Lawrence Ferlinghetti.

Atop Telegraph Hill at **Coit Memorial Tower** ★ (*415-362-0808. Fee for elevator*), you'll enjoy a dazzling view of the city from this 1933 landmark. Across Columbus Avenue rises flower-terraced **Lombard Street** (*Bet. Hyde and Leavenworth Sts.*). Called the "crookedest street in the world," it zigzags nine times down a single steep block.

Now direct yourself to the waterfront. Although the fishing fleet still docks at **Fisherman's Wharf** (*Taylor and Jefferson Sts.*), the biggest fishes landed here now may be tourists, baited by picturesque views over the water and the chance to hook into overpriced seafood dinners. Still, it's fun to eat a walk-away shrimp cocktail, browse the trinket shops, and see such odd attractions as the **Ripley's "Believe It or Not!"** ® **Museum** (*175 Jefferson St. 415-771-6188. Adm. fee*).

Stroll around **Ghirardelli Square,** a 19th-century chocolate factory reborn as shops and restaurants. The nearby **Buena Vista** (*2765 Hyde St. 415-474-5044*) is a classic San Francisco saloon that in 1951 reputedly served the first Irish coffee in America; you know what to order.

Also on the waterfront, the **San Francisco Maritime National Historical Park** ★ (*Beach and Polk Sts. 415-556-3002. Adm. fee to ships*) encompasses a museum full of figureheads and ships-in-bottles, plus historic ships moored at Hyde Street Pier—notably the globe-roaming 1886 square-rigger, *Balclutha.*

Several attractions lie offshore and are accessible from piers. Let your bad-apple imagination roam at **Alcatraz**

Island *(Tours leave from Pier 41. 415-546-2628 for information; 415-546-2700 for advance reservations, which are recommended; fee),* a former federal penitentiary (1934-1963) where Al Capone was a houseguest. You'll see cellblocks, the mess hall, library, and exercise yard; and learn about a tricky, seemingly impossible escape. (See sidebar p. 42.)

More benign is 740-acre **Angel Island State Park** *(415-435-1915. Ferries leave Pier 43 ½. 415-546-2896. Fee).* The

Grant and California Streets, Chinatown

largest island in the bay has felt every footprint of local history—as Native American hunting ground, landfall of the first European to sail through the Golden Gate (Ayala in 1775), cattle ranch, Army post, immigration station, prisoner-of-war camp, and Cold War Nike missile base. Hiking trails wind past historic sites and up to a stunning, 360-degree view of the entire bay area.

Now head west through the Marina District on Marina Boulevard, turning left on Baker Street to the neoclassic **Palace of Fine Arts,** the last remaining structure of the 1915 Panama-Pacific International Exposition. Behind the rotunda stands the **Exploratorium★★** *(3601 Lyon St. 415-563-7337. Daily mid-May–mid-Sept., closed Mon. rest of year; adm. fee).* A cross between mad scientist's lab and penny arcade, it has been rated best science museum in the world by *Scientific American.* Among 650 bleeping, buzzing, hands-on exhibits, you can touch a tornado, find out why your bicycle doesn't have square wheels, blow a bubble bigger than your dog, and leave a shadow image of yourself on the wall.

The city's northwest section has remained a shady wood, thanks to the U.S. Army having maintained a base called the **Presidio** *(Visitor Center, Main Post Bldg. 102 on Montgomery St.*

415-561-4323), founded by Spain in 1776. It's now part of the Golden Gate National Recreation Area. The **Presidio Museum** *(Funston Ave. at Lincoln Blvd. Wed.-Sun.)* has history displays. The adjacent Civil War-era **Fort Point National Historic Site** *(Off Lincoln Blvd. 415-556-1693. Wed.-Sun.)* served as a coastal fortification during World War II. Besides seeing artifacts and cannon drill demonstrations, you have a rare perspective on the Golden Gate Bridge—from underneath.

To see the view from above, take an exhilarating 1.8-mile drive (or walk) across the **Golden Gate Bridge** ★ ★ *(Viewing area off Lincoln Blvd. or US 101),* which spans the entrance to San Francisco Bay.

West of the bridge, via Lincoln Boulevard, stands the **California Palace of the Legion of Honor** ★ ★ *(34th Ave. and Clement St. 415-863-3330. Closed Mon.; adm. fee),* which has ancient and European art from 2500 B.C. through the 20th century, including 70 Rodin sculptures.

The city's green playground, 1,017-acre **Golden Gate Park** *(Bounded by Fulton and Stanyan Sts., Lincoln Way, and Pacific Ocean)* is a place to stroll, paddle a rental boat, remember the sixties' "summer of love," and visit world-class museums. The museums cluster together in the eastern end of the park; enter from Fulton Street on Eighth or Tenth Avenue. The **M.H. de Young Memorial Museum** ★ ★ *(415-863-3330. Wed.-Sun.; adm. fee)* has American masters and traditional arts from Africa, Oceania, and the Americas. The adjacent **Asian Art Museum of San Francisco** ★ ★ *(415-668-8921. Wed.-Sun.; adm. fee),* the world's largest museum devoted to Asian art, encompasses works from 40 countries, including China, India, and Tibet. Close by is the captivating **Japanese Tea Garden,** with its cherry trees and carp ponds; the teahouse reputedly served the first fortune cookie. Across the way, the **California Academy of Sciences** ★ *(415-750-7145. Adm. fee)* embraces a natural history museum, a hall of earth and space sciences (hip-shakin' earthquake simulator and moon rock), an evolution exhibit *(Tyrannosaurus Rex skull),* the **Steinhart Aquarium** (alliga-

Blooming ice plants, near Half Moon Bay

44

tors and dolphins and more),
a planetarium, and a display
of original "Far Side" cartoons.
Other park attractions include
the **Strybing Arboretum and
Botanical Gardens** *(Ninth Ave.
at Lincoln Way. 415-661-0822.
Donation)*; the **Bison Paddock**
(JFK Dr., E of Chain of Lakes Dr.),
opened in 1892 when fewer
than 600 bison survived in the
U.S.; and the **Conservatory of**

Winchester Mystery House, San Jose

Flowers *(JFK Dr. E., near Middle Dr. Closed for renovation).*

Heading south out of San Francisco on 19th Avenue/
Calif. 1, you skirt the ocean and pass through **Pacifica,** the
"fog capital of California." Follow the twists and turns to
Montara State Beach, then go on to ❷ **Half Moon Bay**
(Chamber of Commerce 650-726-5202), known for its pumpkin
fields and the sandy stretch at Half Moon Bay State Beach.

Crossing inland on Calif. 92 offers impressive views of
rolling hills. Then head south on I-280, making a stop in
❸ **Palo Alto** and **Stanford University** *(Sand Hill Rd. exit).
650-723-2560. Guided tours).* Once the horse farm of railroad
magnate Leland Stanford, the 8,180-acre campus is notable
for its Quad, edged with Richardsonian Romanesque sandstone arcades; the 1903 Memorial Church, complete with
biblical mosaics and stained glass; views from Hoover
Tower, which contains Herbert Hoover memorabilia and
an original copy of the *Communist Manifesto;* and the
1-acre Rodin Sculpture Garden.

Continue south on I-280 to ❹ **San Jose** *(Visitor Information 408-977-0900),* founded in 1777 to raise crops for
the nearby presidios of San Francisco and Monterey. The
settlement served as the state's first capital between 1849
and 1851. In the 1960s fruit trees gave way to the indus-
trial parks of Silicon Valley.

Ghosts of the past remain, perhaps literally, at the **Winchester Mystery House**★ *(525 S. Winchester Blvd. 408-247-
2101. Adm. fee),* a strange, 160-room Victorian mansion built
by Sarah Winchester, widow of the firearms heir. According
to legend, a spiritualist medium said she'd live as long as
construction continued—and so it did, around the clock, ·
from 1884 until after she died in 1922. Among the house's
mystifying features are doors that open to blank walls.

Just as mysterious in its way is the **Rosicrucian Egyptian Museum and Planetarium**★ *(Naglee and Park Aves. 408-947-3636. Adm. fee).* Founded by the Rosicrucians (a group that explores the "development of man's unawakened faculties"), it displays mummies of priests, cats, and even a fish; Egyptian jewelry; and a re-created 4,000-year-old rock tomb.

Revitalized in recent years, downtown San Jose is anchored by the **San Jose Museum of Art** *(110 S. Market St. 408-294-2787. Closed Mon.; adm. fee),* devoted to 20th-century works. At the **Tech Museum of Innovation** *(145 W. San Carlos St. 408-279-7150. Closed Mon.; adm. fee),* a robot will make you a (simulated) lunch. You can "fly" over the surface of Mars via computer animation, extract DNA from a cow's

Hills near Livermore

thymus gland, and see how a computer chip is fabricated. Also downtown, the **San Jose Historical Museum** *(Kelley Park, 1600 Senter Rd. 408-287-2290. Adm. fee)* is a 25-acre outdoor collection of historic and re-created buildings, including a fruit barn and corner gas station.

Travel north on I-680, then northeast on Calif. 84, where your surroundings suddenly grow more countrified, with oak trees and horses. In ❺ **Livermore** you can view the world's oldest continuously burning **lightbulb** *(Livermore Fire Dept., 4550 East Ave. 925-373-5450),* aglow since 1901. And there's a cautious optimism to be gained at the **Lawrence Livermore National Laboratory Visitor Center**

46

(N. Greenville Rd. at East Gate Dr. 925-422-6408. Call for hours and tours), with its small exhibit on nuclear fusion, lasers, DNA research, and new materials (including the lightest substance ever made, resembling frozen smoke). Tours visit the world's most powerful laser.

The fertile land around Livermore nurtures a decent wine industry. Two historic wineries to visit are **Concannon Vineyard** *(4590 Tesla Rd. 925-447-3760)* and **Wente Vineyards Estate Winery** *(5565 Tesla Rd. 925-447-3603),* both founded in 1883; the latter is California's oldest continuously operating family winery.

Living history at John Muir N.H.S., Martinez

Follow I-580 and I-680 north to
6 **Danville** *(Diablo Rd. exit to Danville Blvd.),* a sleepy residential town with a Western-style main street full of shops and restaurants. Overlooking golden hills, the **Eugene O'Neill National Historic Site** *(925-838-0249. Wed.-Sun. Tours by reservation)* preserves Tao House, where Eugene O'Neill—the only American playwright to win the Nobel Prize for Literature—wrote such plays as *Long Day's Journey Into Night.*

Across the interstate via Diablo Road, you can stretch your legs on a side trip to **Mount Diablo State Park** ★ *(925-837-2525. Adm. fee),* which encircles the sedimentary rock cone of Mount Diablo (3,849 feet)—not a volcano, although it looks like one. From the top, reached by car or hiking trail, a 360-degree view (on infrequent clear days) sweeps from the Pacific Ocean to the Sierra Nevada. Wildlife includes deer, possums, bobcats, and the rare mountain lion.

If you continue on Diablo Road (which becomes Blackhawk Road), you'll reach the **Blackhawk Automotive Museum** ★ *(3700 Blackhawk Plaza Cir. 925-736-2280. Wed.-Sun.; adm. fee),* which displays a rotating exhibit of one-of-a-kind automobiles—perhaps you'll see the rare 1931 Bugatti Royale, or Lucille Ball's Dual Ghia.

Back on the main route, proceed on I-680 to the city of Walnut Creek, where a spur leads to **Martinez** and the **John Muir National Historic Site** *(4202 Alhambra Ave. 925-228-8860. Wed.-Sun.; adm. fee).* Here is preserved the 1882 Italianate home of writer and naturalist John Muir, who influenced the creation of Yosemite National Park. Just north across Carquinez Strait lies **7** **Benicia** ★ *(Chamber of*

Commerce 707-745-2120), a pleasant waterfront town that proudly served as California's capital in 1853-54. The **Benicia Capitol State Historic Park** *(115 West G St. 707-745-3385. Adm. fee)* contains the state's oldest existing capitol. Next door stands a gold rush hotel that was converted to a private home, the furnished **Fischer-Hanlon House** *(707-745-3385. Guided tours only. Call for schedule; adm. fee).*

From Walnut Creek, the drive continues west on Calif. 24 for about 30 miles to the College Avenue exit. Turn right and head into **Berkeley** *(Convention and Visitors Bureau 510-549-7040 or 800-847-4823),* known best for the university campus that became the proving ground of the 1960s Free Speech Movement. The 30,000-student **University of California at Berkeley** ★ *(E of Oxford St. bet. Bancroft Way and Hearst St. Visitor Center in University Hall, Rm. 101, at Univ. Ave. and Oxford St. 510-642-5215. Tours available)* is renowned for its advanced research and social thought. Among its notable institutions, the **Bancroft Library** has the definitive research collection on the American West; exhibits include the nugget that reputedly started the California Gold Rush. Atop 307-foot **Sather Tower** *(Adm. fee)* awaits a panoramic view of the bay area and the Berkeley Hills. The **University Art Museum** *(2626 Bancroft Way. 510-642-0808. Wed.-Sun.; adm. fee)* features Asian and 20th-century American art, while the adjacent **Pacific Film Archives** *(510-642-1412. Call for schedule; adm. fee)* shows international films. In the hills above the main campus, the **Lawrence Hall of Science** *(Centennial Dr. 510-642-5132. Adm. fee)* has lots of fun, hands-on exhibits that explore the worlds of computers, outer space, animals, and more. For a study break, flop into a chair at any of the coffeehouses near campus.

Sather Gate, University of California at Berkeley

Backtrack to Calif. 24 and continue west to ❽ **Oakland** *(Convention and Visitors Authority 510-839-9000 or 800-262-5526).* At I-580 go southeast to the Grand Avenue exit and take the second right onto Lakeshore Avenue. This busy thoroughfare traces **Lake Merritt,** a natural saltwater lake edged with some 150 acres of paths and gardens.

Follow Lakeshore Avenue around the lake, and turn right on Twelfth Street to the **Oakland Museum of California★★** *(1000 Oak St. 510-238-2200. Wed.-Sun.; adm. fee),* which has three major galleries. One provides a crash course in California history, proceeding from Indian baskets and a gold rush assay office to a pumper from the 1906 San Francisco fire, beatnik coffeehouse, and Apple computer. Another gallery focuses on natural sciences, and the last features artwork from the early 1800s and on, including old photographs, a

Boating on Lake Merritt, Oakland

light-drenched painting of Yosemite Valley by Albert Bierstadt, and 1920s arts and crafts furniture.

Oakland is a port city, whose booming waterfront is lined with nearly 20 miles of berths and terminals. Overlooking the activity you'll find the rather touristy **Jack London Square** *(Foot of Broadway),* named for the writer of *The Call of the Wild,* who spent most of his life in Oakland. Stop by **Heinold's First & Last Chance Saloon** (1883) *(510-839-6761),* where London sold newspapers as a youngster; its floors are slanted from the 1906 quake. The **Jack London Cabin,** moved from the Yukon, is where London lived as a prospector in 1897. At the **Jack London Museum** *(30 Jack London Sq. 510-451-8218. Closed Mon.)* are signed first editions; a model of London's sailboat, the *Snark;* and photos of the author. Docked nearby is the 165-foot-long ***Potomac*** *(510-839-8256. Ship tours April-Oct. Wed. and Sun.; adm. fee. Call for schedule of bay cruises; fare).* A restored former Coast Guard cutter, it served as FDR's floating White House.

The route ends with a crossing of the Bay Bridge, which stretches 4.5 miles in two sections, linked by Yerba Buena Island. You'll be driving on the top deck, affording a panoramic view of San Francisco.

49

Central Coast ★★

● 200 miles ● 2 to 3 days ● Year-round

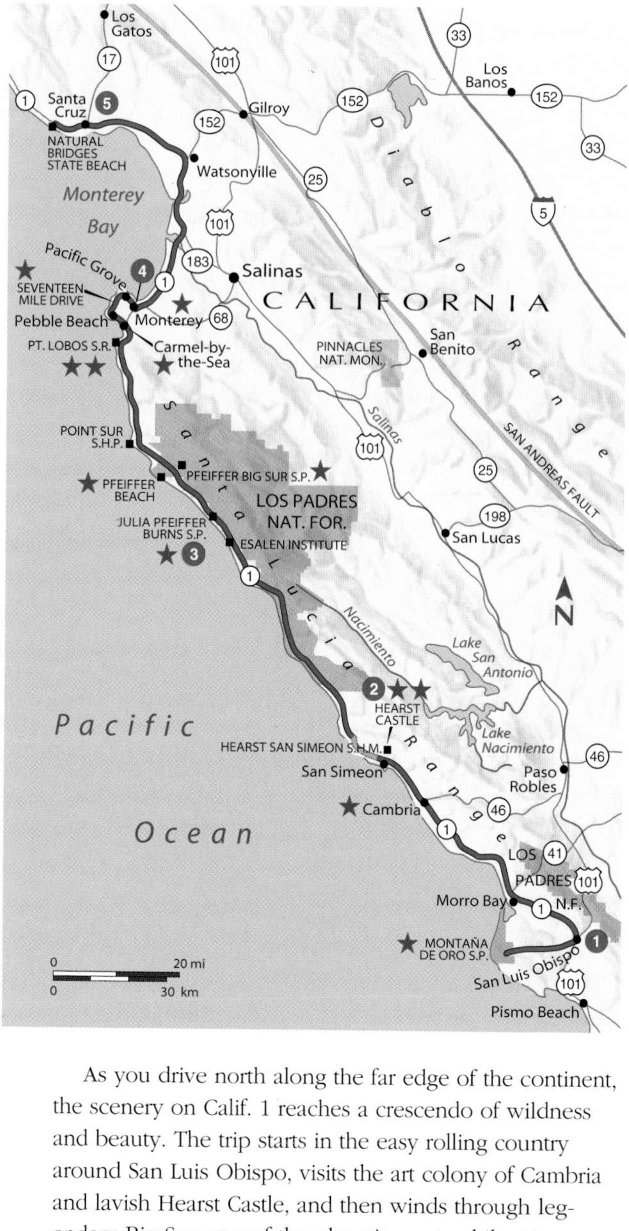

Map labels: Los Gatos · 17 · 101 · 33 · Santa Cruz · 5 · Gilroy · 152 · Los Banos · 152 · NATURAL BRIDGES STATE BEACH · 152 · 33 · Watsonville · 25 · Monterey Bay · 101 · 5 · Pacific Grove · 183 · Salinas · 4 · 1 · SEVENTEEN MILE DRIVE · Pebble Beach · Monterey · 68 · CALIFORNIA · PT. LOBOS S.R. · Carmel-by-the-Sea · PINNACLES NAT. MON. · San Benito · ★★ · POINT SUR S.H.P. · PFEIFFER BIG SUR S.P. · 101 · 25 · SAN ANDREAS FAULT · PFEIFFER BEACH · LOS PADRES NAT. FOR. · 198 · San Lucas · JULIA PFEIFFER BURNS S.P. · ESALEN INSTITUTE · 3 · 1 · Lake San Antonio · Pacific · 2 ★★ · HEARST CASTLE · Lake Nacimiento · HEARST SAN SIMEON S.H.M. · San Simeon · Paso Robles · 46 · Ocean · Cambria · 46 · 1 · LOS PADRES 41 · N.F. · 101 · Morro Bay · 1 · 1 · MONTAÑA DE ORO S.P. · San Luis Obispo · 101 · Pismo Beach

Scale: 0 — 20 mi · 0 — 30 km

N

As you drive north along the far edge of the continent, the scenery on Calif. 1 reaches a crescendo of wildness and beauty. The trip starts in the easy rolling country around San Luis Obispo, visits the art colony of Cambria and lavish Hearst Castle, and then winds through legendary Big Sur, one of the planet's most exhilarating encounters between land and sea. You'll see the village of Carmel, tour old Spanish Monterey, and end up in Santa Cruz, with its surfing beaches and funky-hip lifestyle.

People move at an easy pace in **①** **San Luis Obispo**
(Chamber of Commerce, 1039 Chorro St. 805-781-2777). You'll
see lots of folks riding bikes and skateboards, most likely
students at California Polytechnic State University. The streets
downtown are lined with vintage buildings *(walking tour
brochure available from chamber),* including the 1884 **Ah Louis
Store** *(800 Palm St.),* whose original clientele were mainly
Chinese railroad laborers. In **Bubble Gum Alley** *(Higuera St.
bet. Garden and Broad Sts.),* brick walls are dabbled with wads
of chewing gum that form pictures and spell out names.

Travelers to California soon notice the mission style of
architecture (as evidenced in thick walls, arches, and tile
roofs), the design favored for everything from corporate
headquarters to taco stands. One of the first missions to
use red clay tiles on its roof was the 1772 **Mission San
Luis Obispo de Tolosa** *(Chorro and Monterey Sts. 805-543-
6850. Adm. fee).* The downtown mission is the centerpiece
of a shady plaza on sparkling San Luis Creek, with restaurants and shops nearby.

Also close by, a 1904 Carnegie library houses the **San
Luis Obispo County Historical Museum** *(696 Monterey St.
805-543-0638. Wed.-
Sun.),* with a mail
delivery wagon, cos-
tumed mannequins,
Victorian parlor, and,
among other inter-
esting exhibits, odd
wreaths made of
human hair.

Just south of
town is a kitsch clas-
sic, the **Madonna
Inn** *(100 Madonna
Rd., off US 101. 805-*

Dining room, Madonna Inn

543-3000 or 800-543-9666). Built of stone trimmed in Bar-
bie-doll pink, it holds guest rooms decorated in various
themes, including the ever popular Caveman Room, where
stone walls, a leopard-skin bedspread, and a waterfall
shower await those feeling particularly Neanderthal.

From Madonna Road, follow Los Osos Valley Road to
Montaña de Oro State Park ★ *(Pecho Valley Rd. 805-528-
0513),* whose name, mountain of gold, refers to the color of
sticky monkey flowers that appear here in spring and

summer. The park offers 7 miles of rocky coastline and sandy beach for activities from tide pool rambling to kayaking, plus more than 8,000 acres for hiking, camping, horseback riding, and mountain biking.

Calif. 1 rejoins the ocean north at **Morro Bay** *(Chamber*

Morro Rock, Morrro Bay

of Commerce 805-772-4467 or 800-231-0592), recognizable by its landmark **Morro Rock.** The turban-shaped extinct volcanic peak is perhaps 50 million years old and rises 576 feet. Adjacent **Morro Bay Estuary** contains 2,300 acres of wetlands, eel-grass beds, and mud flats—a home for peregrine falcons, brown pelicans, and great blue herons. In winter, monarch butterflies cluster in eucalyptus trees.

Elephant seals, near San Simeon

Where Monterey pines meet the sea stands the arty village of **Cambria ★** *(Chamber of Commerce 805-927-3624),* about 20 miles north of Morro Bay. The charming eastern section was settled in the 1860s as a center of lumbering, ranching, and whaling. Its Victorian buildings have been dusted off as restaurants, antique shops, and galleries (one of which recently displayed a chair bristling with spikes, titled "No Rest for the Wicked"). Among the offerings of the newer West Village is a toy soldier factory. At nearby **Moonstone Beach** explore tide pools or hunt for moonstones and California

jade. Look for sea otters in the kelp beds offshore.

Heading north beside the Santa Lucia Range, you'll see a gleam on a hilltop — **②** **Hearst Castle** ★★ *(Hearst San Simeon State Historic Monument 805-927-2020 or 800-444-4445. Guided tours only; reservations recommended; adm. fee).* Fabled estate of publisher William Randolph Hearst, its 165 rooms and 127 acres of gardens are open via various tours that visit La Casa Grande and three guesthouses. Prepare to be dizzied by one man's wealth and craving to pile up earthly treasure—Gothic tapestries, Roman mosaics, carved Spanish ceilings, a 5,200-volume library, the Doge's Suite with quatrefoil arches and Venetian decor, a movie theater, and the Neptune pool beside a Greco-Roman temple facade. Yet during Hearst's lavish parties, he had the refectory tables set not only with antique silver, but also common ketchup bottles. Try to take an evening tour offered most Fridays and Saturdays, when docents in 1930s clothes appear as Hearst's famous guests and domestic staff, and a newsreel from the period is shown in the estate's theater.

When you see green ridges plunging into the sea, or perhaps when you see a guy waiting for sunset and playing congas beside an old Volkswagen, you'll know you've reached that mecca of wild beauty and bohemianism, **Big Sur** ★★. This is one of the most scenic stretches of highway in the world. Every curve of the road brings a grand view—headlands melting in fog, redwood canyons, an azure sea foaming against granite rocks.

On the ocean side of Calif. 1 look for **Esalen Institute** *(408-667-3000)*, a New Age-counterculture-human-potential-hot-springs retreat. Then comes a natural high, beautiful **❸** **Julia Pfeiffer Burns State Park** ★ *(831-667-2315. Adm. fee)*, where McWay Falls drops 80 feet into a rocky sea cove. A 6-mile loop trail winds through redwood groves. Five miles ahead lies the **Henry Miller Library** *(831-667-2574)*, which displays books and paintings of the celebrated writer. This lusty personality lived nearby, as recounted in his book, *Big Sur and the Oranges of Hieronymus Bosch.*

Continue to the quintessential Big Sur restaurant, **Nepenthe** ★ *(831-667-2345)*, perched 800 feet above the ocean and overlooking 40 miles of coastline. The name is Greek for a potion that erases sorrow, and a glimpse of the view may do just that. Ahead, make a detour down to see the natural arches and sea stacks of **Pfeiffer Beach** ★ *(2*

Monarch Butterflies of Pacific Grove

Tourists aren't the only ones winging it to Pacific Grove, a charming Victorian settlement on Monterey Bay. Each year from October through March, monarch butterflies flutter in by the thousands. Draped on eucalyptus trees, they remain folded and resemble dead leaves until they're warmed by the morning sun. Then they open their wings and float through the air like pieces from stained-glass windows. The monarchs gather at Washington Park *(Pine and Alder Sts.)* and in a sanctuary on Ridge Road. It seems they are imprinted with a genetic code that passes down from great-grandparents, turning certain generations into rovers that head instinctively for the sanctuary of Pacific Grove. Enjoy their fleeting beauty, fellow travelers.

53

miles off Calif. 1 via Sycamore Canyon Rd.). Treat yourself to a walk along the sandy strand and watch the waves surge into a hole worn through sea-splashed rock. A little farther on at **Pfeiffer Big Sur State Park** ★ *(831-667-2315. Adm. fee),* you can wade in the Big Sur River as it courses among redwoods and ferns, sycamores and cottonwoods. Or hike through the redwoods to Pfeiffer Falls and gaze at its fern-lined grotto. Another trail switchbacks through varying habitat zones to Buzzard's Roost. Other areas lend themselves to picnics and camping.

Farther north, **Point Sur State Historic Park** *(831-625-4419. Guided tours only; call for schedule; adm. fee)* surrounds a light station built in 1889 on a crest of volcanic rock. Soon the road climbs as high as a thousand dizzying feet above the sea, passing over graceful, 714-foot **Bixby Creek Bridge.**

Leave Big Sur behind and, farther along Calif. 1, enter **Point Lobos State Reserve** ★ ★ *(831-624-4909. Adm. fee. No dogs allowed),* a spectacular 1,250-acre chunk of coastline where twisted Monterey cypresses defy the wind on fog-shrouded headlands. Harbor seals and sea lions bask on off-

Neptune pool at Hearst Castle, San Simeon

shore rocks, while cormorants nest on Bird Island and sea otters loll in the seaweed. Dive into the kelp forests of one of the nation's first underwater reserves, or hike the many trails, one leading to an 1850s Chinese fisherman's cabin.

Continue to the almost too-charming village of **Carmel-by-the-Sea**★ *(Visitors Bureau 831-649-1770)*, a former artists' colony that was home to celebrated photographer Ansel Adams. The village—which outlaws neon signs and other modern blights—long ago went upmarket, so bring money to sample the fine restaurants, shops, and art galleries along Ocean Avenue. It's still free to drive along the lanes of fairy-tale cottages and to stroll the crescent of pure white sand that forms the town's front yard.

Most beautiful of all, **Mission San Carlos Borromeo de Carmelo**★★ *(3080 Rio Rd. 831-624-3600. Adm. fee)* manages to transform sandstone into something ineffable. The mission has Moorish towers, a star-shaped window, and walled gardens. Padre Junípero Serra, who administered the mission system from here, lies buried in the sanctuary.

Wildflowers, Big Sur coast

55

The rugged Carmel coast inspired poet Robinson Jeffers to design the **Tor House** *(26304 Ocean View Ave. 831-624-1813. Fri.-Sat. by reservation; adm. fee)* in the early 1900s; it still contains some of his belongings. With his own hands, Jeffers built the adjacent Hawk Tower from stones mainly gathered from the beach below. It was a retreat for his wife and an enchanted place for his sons; note the secret stairway.

Use the Carmel Gate *(off Ocean Ave. on N. San Antonio Ave.)* to enter the **Seventeen Mile Drive**★ *(Adm. fee)*, which runs through the Del Monte Forest and **Pebble Beach.** High points include grand estates such as the Crocker castle, whose private beach is warmed by buried pipes; famous golf links; and offshore rocks teeming with harbor seals and sea lions, squawking gulls and cormorants. The drive also passes the much-photographed Lone Cypress tree, a gnarled symbol of the Monterey Peninsula.

Leave the famed drive at **Pacific Grove,** a popular destination of wintering monarch butterflies (see sidebar page 53). This charming town boasts Victorian architecture; the locally focused **Museum of Natural History** *(Forest and Central Aves. 831-648-3116. Closed Mon.)*; and the Pacific Coast's oldest continuously operating lighthouse, the 1855 **Point Pinos Lighthouse** *(Asilomar Ave. 831-648-3116. Thurs.-Sun.)*.

Follow Ocean View Boulevard east into ❹ **Monterey** ★ *(Visitor Centers, 380 Alvarado St. and 401 Camino El Estero. 831-649-1770).* The flags of Spain, Mexico, and the United States have all flown over this handsome city, and since the late 1800s it has flourished as a tourist destination.

Along Monterey Bay sprawls **Cannery Row** *(Obtain walking tour map at railroad car, 65 Prescott St.),* the heart of the sardine-canning industry that thrived here from the 1920s to the 1950s. The haunt of hard-living characters, the row was immortalized by John Steinbeck in his 1945 book, *Cannery Row,* as "a poem, a stink, a grating noise, a quality of light, a tone, a habit . . . a dream." In the late 1940s, sardines began to vanish, prompting marine biologist Ed Ricketts (who inspired Steinbeck's main character, Doc) to quip: "They're all in cans." Ricketts's old Pacific Biological Laboratory still stands *(800 Cannery Row),* but tourism has taken over the row, with shops flogging T-shirts and taffy.

Kelp forest, Monterey Bay Aquarium

At the district's west end, the technologically advanced **Monterey Bay Aquarium** ★ ★ *(886 Cannery Row. 831-648-4888. Adm. fee)* acts as an extension of the bay just outside. It displays 360,000 creatures, from delicate jellyfish to roving sharks. Look through the world's biggest window (15 feet high and 54 feet long) at the Outer Bay exhibit, a million-gallon indoor ocean that's home to sunfish (which can be 10 feet tall and weigh 3,000 pounds), green sea turtles, and schools of tuna. Also intriguing are the three-story kelp forest and the ever playful sea otters.

Downtown, yesterday lives on at **Monterey State Historic Park** ★ *(Custom House Plaza. 831-649-7118).* Get your bearings, see a historical video, and pick up a brochure or join a guided walking tour at **Stanton Center.** Here, too, is the **Maritime Museum of Monterey** *(831-373-2469),* which displays model ships, Chinese junks, and antique sextants. A few steps away is the oldest public building in California, the adobe **Custom House** (circa 1827), heaped with cargo of early days.

Scattered around town, the park's other historic structures include **Colton Hall** *(522 Pacific St. 831-646-3851),* where delegates wrote California's first constitution in 1849; the **Larkin House** *(510 Calle Principal. Closed Tues. and Thurs.;*

adm. fee), begun in 1835, which blends Yankee and Mexican architecture in the Monterey colonial style; the farm and residence buildings of the mid-1800s **Cooper-Molera Complex** *(525 Polk St. Closed Mon.; adm. fee);* the **Robert Louis Stevenson House** *(530 Houston St. Closed Mon. and Wed.),* which contains memorabilia of the Scottish storyteller, a boarder in 1879; and the 1795 **Royal Presidio Chapel** *(Church and Figueroa Sts.),* Monterey's oldest building.

Continue north on Calif. 1 to the beach town of ❺ **Santa Cruz** *(Visitor Center 831-425-1234 or 800-833-3494),* whose mild climate results partly from sheltering mountains. You'll see the peace sign flashed regularly in this woodsy home of University of California students and counterculture dropouts. Along the ocean, fun-seekers will enjoy the **Santa Cruz Beach Boardwalk ★** *(831-423-5590. Daily in summer, closed Dec., weekends and holidays rest of year; fee for rides).* The 28 rides include the Giant Dipper wooden roller coaster, built in 1924.

Santa Cruz Beach Boardwalk

Bait shops and seafood restaurants line the nearby half-mile-long **Santa Cruz Municipal Wharf,** while sandy beaches meet the ocean below. Check out a top surfing spot, Steamer Lane, at the foot of the cliffs below the **Santa Cruz Surfing Museum** *(Inside lighthouse on W. Cliff Dr. 831-429-3429. Closed Tues.).* Surfing began in California in 1886, when two Hawaiian princesses came to Santa Cruz and had redwood surfboards milled for them. Inside the museum are a multitude of surfboards ranging from the 1920s to today's high-tech short boards, including one with teeth marks from an attack by a great white shark.

Farther along West Cliff Drive lies **Natural Bridges State Beach** *(831-423-4609. Parking fee),* named for a wave-cut rock formation offshore. There are good tide pools and, between October and March, one of the nation's largest populations of overwintering monarch butterflies. The Visitor Center holds nature exhibits.

Finally, for older history visit **Santa Cruz Mission S.H.P.** *(144 School St. 831-425-5849. Thurs.-Sun.; adm. fee),* containing the only building left from the original mission. It now holds a museum focusing on Native Americans and Californios.

Santa Barbara Loop★

● 166 miles ● 2 days ● Year-round

This sunny romp starts in Santa Barbara, a coastal resort where bougainvillea flowers climb white walls and an old California mission drowses in the sun. Among the city's ravishing charms are a Mediterranean climate, gardens, broad beaches, a pretty yacht harbor, and mountains tinged with impressionist pinks and blues. Leaving here, the drive makes two loops. First it jogs westward, visiting the flower fields of sleepy Lompoc and the wine and horse country of the newly glamorous Santa Ynez Valley. Then, circling back to Santa Barbara, it takes off eastward, to the mission city of Ventura and the orange groves of the Ojai Valley.

❶ Santa Barbara★★ (*Visitor Information 805-965-3021*) was settled by the Spanish in the late 1700s and lived graciously during California's later *rancho* period. In the late 19th century, it became a health resort for wealthy Easterners after a guidebook writer touted it as a "Mecca for the moribund." When a 1925 earthquake leveled the haphazardly built, cluttered downtown, far-sighted civic leaders rebuilt in the Spanish colonial style that now unifies the city.

On a slope overlooking town stands venerable **Mission Santa Bárbara★★** (*2201 Laguna St. 805-682-4713. Adm. fee*). At the old mission, founded in 1786, it's easy to picture gray-robed padres saying Mass for the Indians (who, since there were no pews, sat on the floor).

Franciscan friars still reside at this Queen of the Missions, and Sunday services continue in the colorfully painted church. The sandstone Roman facade and adobe walls demonstrate how missionaries integrated European architecture with the rude but handsome materials available on the California frontier: mud, stone, and timber.

From here, head up Mission Canyon. Kids love the **Santa Barbara Museum of Natural History** ★ *(2559 Puesta del Sol Rd. 805-682-4711. Adm. fee),* with its 72-foot blue whale skeleton, animal dioramas, insects, "lizard lounge," and planetarium. The tree-shaded grounds by Mission Creek make a lovely picnic spot. At the nearby **Santa Barbara Botanic Garden** *(1212 Mission Canyon Rd. 805-682-4726. Adm. fee)* miles of paths wind among a thousand species of California native plants, from paper-dry poppies to fog-loving redwood trees. A dam across the creek was built by padres and Chumash Indians in 1806.

Arlington Theatre, downtown Santa Barbara

Downtown, take in a movie or concert at the **Arlington Theatre** *(1317 State St. 805-963-4408. Adm. fee)* just to see the interior, designed to evoke the plaza of a Spanish village. At the nearby **Santa Barbara Museum of Art** ★ *(1130 State St. 805-963-4364. Closed Mon.; adm. fee except Thurs.),* look for Monet's 1884 painting of the Italian Riviera in sunny pastels; it could have been painted yesterday in Santa Barbara. This impressive regional museum also has works by Matisse and Chagall, Hopper and O'Keeffe, plus classical antiquities and Asian art.

Wander a few blocks to the **Santa Barbara County Courthouse** ★★ *(1100 Anacapa St. 805-962-6464. Tours Mon.-Sat.),* which looks like a fantasy out of *El Cid.* Built in 1929, it has thick white walls and red-tile roofs, set off by sunken gardens. Inside are hand-painted ceilings, wrought-iron chandeliers, hallways sheathed in Tunisian tiles, and marvelous historical murals. For a 360-degree view of the city, ride the elevator up the clock tower.

Nearby, **El Presidio de Santa Barbara State Historic Park** *(123 E. Canon Perdido St. 805-966-9719)* preserves a bit of Spain's original military outpost, including the city's oldest remaining building (1788), which once provided housing for married soldiers and their families. Reconstruction of the fort includes an adobe chapel, a two-story lookout tower, and soldiers' and commander's quarters.

The **Santa Barbara Historical Society Museum** *(136 E. De la Guerra St. 805-966-1601. Closed Mon.)*, a short stroll away, displays iron treasure chests from Spanish explorers, silver saddles from the *rancho* period, and a golden altar from old Chinatown. Material from Santa Barbara's Flying A Studio, which pioneered moviemaking around 1913 and became the then-largest studio in the world, includes the eighth Bell-and-Howell motion picture camera ever made.

Stearns Wharf, Santa Barbara

A charming holdover from earlier days is the nearby 1920s shopping arcade called **El Paseo** *(State and De la Guerra Sts.)*, which calls to mind a street in Spain. Passages wind among shops built around the adobe 1828 **Casa de la Guerra** *(Closed to the public)*, the home of the Spanish military commander and the center of Santa Barbara's surprisingly refined society of the 1820s.

Now turn toward the city's waterfront, where **Stearns Wharf** *(Foot of State St.)* ranks as the oldest wharf operating on the West Coast (1872). Like any self-respecting pier, it has a bait shop and a gypsy palm reader; also, restaurants and shops. The **Sea Center** *(211 Stearns Wharf. 805-962-0885. Adm. fee)* displays a model whale and tanks of live marine animals, giving you a glimpse (and sometimes a feel) of what's underwater in the Santa Barbara Channel. **Santa Barbara Harbor★** is both a yacht basin and a real working port. Inhale the waterfront smells of boiling crabs, diesel fuel, and salt spray; walk to the end of the breakwater for a memorable view of the ocean, mountains, and town. **Whale-watching trips** *(Sea Landing. 805-963-3564. Fee)* seek blue whales and humpbacks June through September, and gray whales December through May.

Just east of the wharf you'll find **East Beach**—the most popular of Santa Barbara's 5 miles of **beaches★★.** Here, volleyball players dive for impossible shots, young women wear impossible bikinis, and young men look as if they walked out of *GQ* magazine.

Leave Santa Barbara on US 101 north, passing **El Capitan, Refugio,** and **Gaviota beaches** before the route turns inland. At Gaviota Pass the surroundings change from coastal grasslands to chaparral with sycamore trees. A few miles north of the junction with Calif. 1, a side trip leads to **Nojoqui Falls** *(Old Coast Hwy. to Alisal Rd. Nojoqui Falls County Park 805-688-4217)*, which cascades—or trickles, depending on the season—down a cliff of sandstone and shale that is draped in maidenhair ferns.

Backtrack to Calif. 1 and head north through rolling hills sprinkled with oaks and cows to **2** **Lompoc** *(Chamber of Commerce, 111 South I St. 805-736-4567 or 800-240-0999. Field maps available)*. Nicknamed the Valley of the Flowers, this region produces up to 75 percent of the world's flower seeds. In June and July hundreds of acres bloom with asters, zinnias, petunias, and marigolds. Roll down your car window to catch the heavenly fragrance of sweet peas.

Calif. 246 leads east to **La Purísima Mission State Historic Park** ★ ★ *(2295 Purisima Rd. 805-733-3713. Adm. fee)*. No other California mission so hauntingly evokes the era of the Spanish padres. Situated in the hills beyond sight of modern life, the perfectly restored mission has a painted church, workshops, residences, fountains, and gardens. Ask about the fine living history events.

Flower beds near Lompoc

Keep going to **3** **Solvang** *(Visitors Bureau 805-688-6144)*, a relentlessly quaint village that capitalized on its founding by Danes in 1911 by later adopting a Danish look to attract tourists. It's all half-timbered architecture, clock towers, fluttering flags, Scandinavian bakeries, and gift shops. The **Hans Christian Andersen Museum** *(1680 Mission Dr. 805-688-2052)* has displays on the Danish writer's life and first editions of his work. On the town's east side stands the 1804 **Mission Santa Inés** *(1760 Mission Dr. 805-688-4815. Adm. fee)*, whose museum displays old crucifixes, musical instruments, and fine 16th-century vestments.

Drive on into the **Santa Ynez Valley** ★, where horse ranchers raise fine Arabians, Andalusians, paints, and Icelandics. Miniature horses, no taller than 34 inches, roam **Quicksilver Farm** *(1555 Alamo Pintado Rd., near Solvang).* Numerous wineries throughout the valley offer tours and tastings, notably of Chardonnay *(winery map available at Santa Barbara County Vintners' Assoc., 3669 Sagunto St., Santa Ynez. 805-688-0881 or 800-218-0881).*

Stop at tiny **Santa Ynez** and mosey past false-fronted buildings that look like sets for a cowboy movie. A Wells Fargo stagecoach and other rolling antiques are parked at the **Santa Ynez Valley Historical Society Museum and Carriage House** *(3596 Sagunto St. 805-688-7889. Museum Fri.-Sun., carriage house closed Mon.).* See Chumash and pioneer artifacts, plus an 1895 jailhouse whose inmates were sometimes allowed to "escape" at night, returning in the morning.

Now drive Calif. 154 toward Santa Barbara. You'll pass **Cachuma Lake Recreation Area** *(805-686-5054. Adm. fee),* a liquid blue mirage amid the dry hills. It offers fishing, boating, and camping, but no swimming (the lake is residential drinking water). In summer a naturalist guides boat tours *(fee)* to view ospreys, deer, great blue herons, and turtles.

Mission Santa Inés, near Solvang

After cresting the Santa Ynez Mountains, detour into history at **Chumash Painted Cave State Historic Park** *(2 miles E on Painted Cave Rd.; road not suitable for trailers or RVs),* where more than two centuries ago Chumash Indian shamans painted pictographs on cave walls, probably for religious use. Yet no one knows the meaning of the wheels and other colorful but fading symbols.

The drive returns to Santa Barbara and commences the second loop, heading south on US 101. Just east of town lies **Montecito** ★, a residential enclave where millionaires and movie stars dwell on estates built around the turn of the century. Drive along the lanes to see Tudor mansions, Spanish haciendas, and Italian villas.

About 20 miles farther along US 101 you'll reach ❹ **Ventura** *(Visitors Bureau 805-648-2075 or 800-333-2989).* Downtown, history buffs will enjoy the small **San Buenaventura Mission and Museum** *(211 E. Main St. 805-643-4318. Donation),* founded by Padre Junípero Serra in 1782. The nearby **Ventura County Museum of History and Art**

(100 E. Main St. 805-653-0323. Closed Mon.; adm. fee) has costumed historical miniature figures, Chumash artifacts, and early agricultural machines.

At Ventura Harbor is the **Channel Islands National Park Visitor Center** *(1901 Spinnaker Dr. 805-658-5730),* whose tide pool display and other exhibits focus on the park's five islands—Anacapa, Santa Cruz, Santa Rosa, San Miguel, and Santa Barbara—and the surrounding marine sanctuary. Take a day or overnight excursion to the **Channel Islands National Park ★** *(Island Packers, 1867 Spinnaker Dr. 805-642-7688 or 805-642-1393. Fare)* to hike, camp, kayak, scuba dive, and view sea lions and indigenous foxes. You'll discover a world that hints of California in the early 1800s. In season, whale-watching boats head out to view blue, humpback, and gray whales.

Topiary art, Ojai

Now follow Calif. 33 north to the Ojai Valley town of
5 Ojai ★ *(Visitors Bureau 805-646-8126),* long a mecca for the metaphysically inclined. In an old chapel downtown, the **Ojai Valley Museum** *(130 W. Ojai Ave. 805-646-2290)* displays the relics of Chumash Indians and early settlers. A nearby local institution is **Bart's Books** *(302 W. Matilija St. 805-646-3755. Closed Mon.),* a rambling shop with an honor system for after-hours customers; simply choose a book from the outside shelves and drop the money through a door slot.

63

Be sure to explore the Ojai Valley's east end. With its palm-lined lanes and citrus groves, set against the mountains, the scene looks like a vintage orange-crate label. Out here, the **Krishnamurti Library** *(1130 McAndrew Rd. 805-646-4948. Closed Mon.-Tues.)* has books and videotapes of renowned Indian spiritual figure Jiddu Krishnamurti, who lived on and off for

Santa Ynez Mountains, north of Santa Barbara

more than six decades in this 1895 California ranch house.

To finish the drive, take scenic Calif. 150 past **Lake Casitas,** popular with fishermen and boaters, then across mountains of sandstone and chaparral. On reaching US 101 swing north to Santa Barbara.

Los Angeles to the

● **125 miles** ● **2 to 3 days** ● **Year-round** ● **Beware of maniacal motorists on the more than 500 miles of L.A. area freeways.**

LOS ANGELES AREA

Burbank

NBC STUDIOS
WARNER BROS. STUDIOS **7**
Universal City
UNIVERSAL STUDIOS ★★ HOLLYWOOD
HIGHLAND AVE.
★ ★ MANN'S CHINESE THEATRE
HOLLYWOOD BLVD.
4 Hollywood BLVD.
BEVERLY HILLS HOTEL ★
SUNSET
Beverly Hills **3** ★
RODEO DRIVE
5 FARMERS MARKET
LOS ANGELES COUNTY MUSEUM OF ART ★
MUSEUM OF TOLERANCE ■
6
To Santa Monica Venice, & Malibu
Culver City
405

ALAMEDA AVE.
GOLDEN STATE FWY.
VENTURA
★ LOS ANGELES ZOO
Glendale
GRIFFITH PARK
HOLLYWOOD STUDIO MUSEUM
GRIFFITH OBSERVATORY & PLANETARIUM
LOS FELIZ BLVD.
SANTA MONICA BLVD.
RANCHO LA BREA TAR PITS/ GEORGE C. PAGE MUSEUM
PETERSEN AUTOMOTIVE MUSEUM ★
WILSHIRE BLVD.
MUSEUM OF CONTEMPORARY ART ■
BRADBURY BLDG.
EXPOSITION BLVD.
EXPOSITION PARK
110

AUTRY MUSEUM OF WESTERN HERITAGE ★
FWY.
GLENDALE AVE.
STATE FWY.
SUNSET
BLVD.
PASADENA
EL PUEBLO DE LOS ANGELES H.M. & OLVERA STREET
UNION STATION ★
1
★ ★ **Los Angeles** ★ ★
GEFFEN CONTEMPORARY
5
CENTRAL AVE.
GRAND AVE.
WESTERN AVE.
ALVARADO ST.

ARROYO BLVD.
ROSE BOWL ■
★ ★ GAMBLE HOUSE ■
8 ★
Pasadena
COLORADO BLVD.
NORTON SIMON MUSEUM ★ ★
HUNTINGTON LIBRARY, ART COLLECTIONS, AND BOTANICAL GARDENS ■
★ ★
FOREST LAWN MEMORIAL PARK
South Pasadena
SOUTHWEST MUSEUM ■ **2**
HUNTINGTON DR.
VALLEY BLVD.
Alhambra
BLVD.
10
ATLANTIC
710
60
WHITTIER BLVD.
To Arcadia
210

0 ___ 4 mi
0 ___ 6 km

64

This drive starts in Los Angeles and heads west to a celebrity register of spots to "see and be seen": Hollywood, Beverly Hills, Venice. It then moves eastward through the pleasant Pasadena area to two mountain lakes, Arrowhead and Big Bear. You'll quickly observe that the City of Angels has its heavenly side (sunshine, a feeling of unlimited possibilities and vitality), and its devils (smog, traffic, and tensions that hint of menace). This makes L.A. at once fascinating and frightening, a great sprawling mixed message. Geographically, it's the hub of one of the nation's largest metropolitan areas, measuring about 34,000 square miles. (To see the Los Angeles basin at its prettiest, drive into the hills at night, when the grid of streets below creates a glowing plane geometry.) Sociologically, L.A. is a place that continually re-invents itself, launching trends in entertainment and lifestyles. Sample L.A.'s multiethnic culture, smile at its starstruck silliness—and enjoy the ride.

Start exploring **Los Angeles** ★ ★ *(Visitor Information 213-689-8822 or 800-228-2452)* in the heart of downtown at **1** **El Pueblo de Los Angeles Historic Monument** *(Between*

Alameda, Arcadia, and Spring Sts., and Cesar E. Chavez Ave. Visitor Center at Sepulveda House, 622 N. Main St. 213-628-1274).
When 11 farming families from Mexico settled a pueblo
in 1781, they sowed the seeds of today's metropolitan
area of over 15 million people. Still standing are the
city's oldest house (Avila Adobe, 1818), first firehouse,
and first church. The tourist-oriented **Olvera Street** re-
creates a Mexican marketplace, with historic buildings,
handicraft stalls, and spicy food.

Hollywood Walk of Fame

Visit nearby **Union Station**★ *(800 N. Alameda St.)*
for its classic California architecture, a mix of Spanish
colonial revival with streamline moderne. Another
downtown institution is the **Museum of Contemporary Art**★ *(250 S. Grand Ave. 213-626-6222. Closed
Mon.; adm. fee includes entrance to Geffen Contemporary)*,
a bold cluster of geometric buildings and subter-
ranean galleries that display *very* contemporary work. Affili-
ated shows are mounted at the nearby **Geffen
Contemporary** *(152 N. Central Ave. 213-626-6222. Closed Mon.;
adm. fee includes entrance to Museum of Contemporary Art)*.

65

To get a feeling for elegant Victorian commerce, have
a peek at the marble and tile in the nearby 1893 **Bradbury Building** *(304 S. Broadway. 213-626-1893. Closed Sun.)*.
The atrium is illuminated by a skylight,
and each surrounding floor is filigreed
with wrought-iron railings.

Along the Pasadena Freeway (Calif.
110) northeast of downtown stands the
② **Southwest Museum**★ *(234 Museum
Dr. 323-221-2164. Closed Mon.; adm. fee)*. The
fun way to enter Los Angeles's oldest
museum (1914) is through a tunnel inside
Mount Washington and via an elevator to
the galleries. The collection's quarter-of-a-
million artifacts are drawn from California
(Chumash serpentine bowls), the Southwest (Navajo blankets), the Plains (Lakota
beaded tobacco bags), and the Northwest
coast (Tlingit wool tunics).

Los Angeles at night

South of the downtown core in Exposition Park sprawls the **Natural History
Museum of Los Angeles County**★ *(900
Exposition Blvd. 213-744-3466. Closed Mon.; adm. fee)*. Bring
your jogging shoes to explore this vast repository of 35

million items. Taken from nature and history, they vary from dinosaurs to diamonds, Egyptian mummies to stuffed birds to Hollywood memorabilia. Also in Exposition Park, the **California Museum of Science and Industry** *(700 State Dr. 213-744-7400)* uses hands-on exhibits to juggle ideas in science, health, and space. Try to take in a show at the eye-popping big-screen IMAX theater *(adm. fee)*.

Now drive west along Wilshire Boulevard to ❸ **Rancho La Brea Tar Pits/George C. Page Museum**★ *(5801 Wilshire Blvd. 323-936-2230. Museum closed Mon.; adm. fee)*. Bones of Ice Age animals, such as saber-toothed cats and mammoths, have been plucked from these gas-belching pools of gummy asphalt where the unfortunate critters were trapped about 35,000 years ago. The adjacent museum showcases Pleistocene skeletons and a working paleontology lab—don't miss the display in which a saber-toothed cat seems to melt away to bones.

The extensive holdings at the nearby **Los Angeles County Museum of Art**★ *(5905 Wilshire Blvd. 323-857-6000. Closed Mon.; adm. fee)* cover the gamut from pre-Columbian gold to European Renaissance paintings and 20th-century American art. Also of note are the excellent collections of Roman glass, costumes, and Japanese art.

Roll down memory lane on a tour of the automobile in southern California history, across the street at the **Petersen Automotive Museum**★ *(6060 Wilshire Blvd. 323-930-2277. Closed Mon.; adm. fee)*. Cars are displayed in period settings—a 1931 dealer's showroom, a 1957 drive-in restaurant, a 1960 suburban garage, and so on.

Giant guitar, Universal Studios

Stroll just a few blocks to the **Farmers Market** *(3rd St. and Fairfax Ave. 323-933-9211)*, a beloved L.A. landmark dating from 1934. This open-air market sells fresh produce and corny California souvenirs (salt 'n' pepper shakers shaped like oranges, anyone?). The walk-up restaurants offer international menus and a reasonable chance of spotting Hollywood celebs noshing.

North of downtown lies **Griffith Park** *(Entrances from I-5, Calif. 134, or Los Feliz Blvd.)*, at 4,107 acres one of America's largest municipal parks. Here you can hike, ride a carousel or miniature train, and visit three worthwhile institutions. At the northern end of Vermont Avenue, **Griffith Observatory & Planetarium** *(323-664-1191. Sept.-May closed*

Mon.) offers free telescope viewing on clear nights and planetarium/laser-light shows *(adm. fee)* in the copper dome. The art deco observatory was a location in the 1955 film *Rebel Without A Cause* with James Dean. Come back to earth at the **Los Angeles Zoo**★ *(5333 Zoo Dr. 323-666-4090. Adm. fee),* where more than 1,200 animals are arranged by continent. The **Autry Museum of Western Heritage**★ *(4700 Western Heritage Way. 323-667-2000. Closed Mon.; adm. fee)* looks at the Wild West—both its history and its romanticized portrayal by Hollywood. See William "Buffalo Bill" Cody's saddle and Annie Oakley's gold pistol, and grow nostalgic over a child's bedroom furnished entirely in 1950s Hopalong Cassidy gear—an example of early television product licensing.

Now head for ❹ **Hollywood** *(Visitor Center 213-236-2331),* the place about which pianist Oscar Levant quipped, "Strip away the phony tinsel...and you'll find the real tinsel underneath." First stop: **Hollywood Boulevard.** This thoroughfare of Hollywood's golden age is sadly tarnished now, its old-time glamour dulled. But plenty of tourists mingle with the tattooed teenagers lounging on littered corners along the **Walk of Fame,** where showbiz names (some you recognize, some you've hardly even heard of) are inscribed in brass-trimmed pink terrazzo stars in the sidewalk.

Do visit **Mann's Chinese Theatre**★★ *(6925 Hollywood Blvd. 323-464-8111),* a pagoda of green roofs and dragons opened by showman Sid Grauman in 1927 with a premiere of Cecil B. DeMille's *King of Kings.* In the famous forecourt, check whether your shoes fit the concrete footprints of stars from Mary Pickford to John Travolta. Not far away, the small but interesting **Hollywood Studio Museum**★ *(2100 N. Highland Ave. 323-874-2276. Sat.-Sun.; adm. fee)* occupies a horse barn where fledgling director Cecil B. DeMille shot Hollywood's first feature western, *The Squaw Man,*

On Venice Beach

in 1913. Among relics of the silent era are the chariot from the 1926 *Ben Hur* and Mary Pickford's makeup case.

If you yearn to see movie stars in the flesh, go west to where they live — ❺ **Beverly Hills** *(Visitors Bureau 310-248-1010 or 800-345-2210).* Mingle with celebs in the luxury boutiques on world-famous **Rodeo Drive,** or watch Hollywood dealmakers schmooze in the famous Polo Lounge at the perennially pink **Beverly Hills**

Hotel★ *(9641 Sunset Blvd. 310-276-2251).*

On the west side of Los Angeles, the **Museum of Tolerance**★ *(9786 W. Pico Blvd. 310-553-8403. Closed Sat.; adm. fee. Reservations available)* uses interactive exhibits to convey a piercing experience of racism and prejudice, from ethnic cleansing in Bosnia to the continuing struggle for civil rights in America. Encounters include a walk back in time to the Holocaust of World War II. Holocaust survivors speak to visitors of their experiences three times a day. You leave the museum not depressed, but inspired to make a positive difference in the world.

Drive west as far as you can without falling in the ocean, and you're in ❻ **Santa Monica** *(Visitor Center 310-393-7593),* with its art gallery scene and miles of beaches. On the **Santa Monica Pier** *(End of Colorado Ave.)* is a 1916 carousel (featured in the movie *The Sting),* roller coaster, and bumper cars for those who can't get enough of rush-hour traffic.

Hollywood automobile

Atop the nearby bluffs along Ocean Avenue, try **Palisades Park** for a sunset stroll. On the east side of town, the **Museum of Flying**★ *(Santa Monica Airport, Ocean Park Blvd. and 28th St. 310-392-8822. Wed.-Sun.; adm. fee)* displays vintage Douglas aircraft, including the World Cruiser that made the first round-the-globe flight in 1924.

Just south is **Venice** *(Visitor information 213-689-8822),* a seaside showcase of southern California culture at its kookiest. The **Venice Boardwalk**★ *(Ocean Front Walk bet. Navy St. and Venice Blvd.)* has a carnival atmosphere—jugglers passing the hat, musclemen hoisting barbells, and lots of skaters. Partially restored canals and bridges *(E of Pacific Ave. and S of Venice Blvd.)* were meant to evoke Venice, Italy, in the neighborhood's original development in 1905.

If you drive north on the Pacific Coast Highway (Calif. 1) from Santa Monica, you'll reach the **J. Paul Getty Museum**★★ *(17985 Pacific Coast Hwy., just S of Malibu. 310-458-2003. Closed Mon. Parking by reservation only. Note: Getty Malibu museum closed 1997-2000 for renovation; portion of collection will be at new Getty Center in West L.A. Call for updated information.).* The oil billionaire's legacy is a replica of a 2,000-year-old Roman country villa, which he

Map labels:
ANGELES NAT. FOR. San Gabriel Mountains Big Pines 138 15 138 18 10 mi 15 km 18
San Fernando 118 5 CREST 2 HWY. ANGELES 210 RIM OF THE WORLD SCENIC BYWAY 173 Lake Arrowhead Big Bear Lake 10
CALIF. ★ 9 San Bernardino 18 18 38 Big Bear Lake
101 27 101 101 7 134 2 8 Pasadena Arcadia 210 30 10 San Bernardino 30 SAN ANDREAS FAULT 215 SAN BERNARDINO N.F. see p. 76
Malibu Los Angeles WARNER BROS. STUDIOS San Marino 60 Pomona Redlands 10 Banning
Santa Monica 6 Venice Pacific Ocean 1 10 110 710 5 605 57 60 15 91 Riverside 60 243

landscaped authentically and filled with remarkable
antiquities from Greece and Rome—vases, sculptures, and
mosaics. Among the other treasures are European paintings such as van Gogh's "Irises," drawings, decorative art,
and medieval manuscripts.

Now take the scenic Topanga Canyon Boulevard
(Calif. 27) to US 101 to that moviemaking mecca, **Universal Studios Hollywood★★** *(100 Universal Plaza, Universal
City. 818-508-9600. Adm. fee).* A tram tour takes you
through one of Los Angeles's largest studios, which dou-
bles as a theme park. Big attractions include the $120 mil-
lion *Jurassic Park* ride, an attack by the toothy *Jaws* shark,
a cowboy stunt show, and the heart-pounding *Back to the
Future* ride aboard a flight simulator.

Next, follow the Ventura Freeway (Calif. 134) east to the
❼ **Warner Bros. Studios** *(Hollywood Way and Olive Ave., Burbank. 818-972-8687. Mon.-Fri.; adm.
fee. Reservations recommended. No
children under age ten).* Tours
explain the nuts-and-bolts of creating films and TV shows, with visits
to prop and wardrobe depart-
ments, soundstages, and sound-
effects studios. For a look behind
the scenes at a television studio
and the world of sets, makeup, and
"blue screen" technology, visit the
NBC Studios *(3000 W. Alameda Ave,
Burbank. 818-840-3537. Mon.-Fri.; adm. fee).* Call for free ticket
information to watch a taping of *The Tonight Show.*

J. Paul Getty Museum, near Malibu

Continue eastward on the Ventura Freeway, past
Forest Lawn Memorial Park in Glendale (see sidebar
next page), to ❽ **Pasadena★** *(Visitor Center 626-795-9311),*
a city of tree-lined streets against a backdrop of the San

Los Angeles to the Mountains

Forest Lawn Memorial Park

In Glendale, visit **Forest Lawn Memorial Park** (1712 S. Glendale Ave. 213-254-3131 or 800-204-3131), one place where you're sure to be near movie stars; they're buried here. Look for Clark Gable, Carole Lombard, and Walt Disney. The grounds are scattered with 300 marble statues and reproduction artworks, including a stained-glass version of Leonardo's "Last Supper." The cemetery's ostentatious reverence and hands-clasped hype helped inspire Evelyn Waugh's 1948 novel, *The Loved One*, a parody of American funerary culture.

Gabriel Mountains. You've seen it on television on New Year's Day during the Tournament of Roses Parade—which began in 1890 as a public relations gimmick to promote the city's sunny winter weather. The **Rose Bowl** (1001 Rose Bowl Dr. off Arroyo Blvd.), which plays host to the popular college football game on New Year's Day, also serves as a mammoth flea market (second Sun. of the month).

In town stands one of America's great residences, the **Gamble House**★★ (4 Westmoreland Pl. 626-793-3334. Thurs.-Sun.; adm. fee). Built for a family that co-founded Procter & Gamble, the shingled house was constructed in 1908 by architects Greene and Greene, masters of the arts and crafts style. Its exquisite interior comprises 17 kinds of wood, and is decorated with Tiffany lamps and custom-made furniture.

An array of European masterpieces from Rembrandt and Goya to van Gogh and Cézanne (not to mention more than 70 Degas bronzes) are on display at the nearby **Norton Simon Museum**★★ (411 W. Colorado Blvd. 626-449-6840. Thurs.-Sun.; adm. fee). The museum also holds an impressive Asian sculpture collection.

Adjacent San Marino claims a world-class cultural institution, the **Huntington Library, Art Collections, and Botanical Gardens**★★ (1151 Oxford Rd. 626-405-2141. Closed Mon.; adm. fee), founded by rail magnate Henry E. Huntington. Bibliophiles will gaze in awe at rare manuscripts and books that include an illuminated *Canterbury Tales* (circa 1410), a Gutenberg Bible, early Shakespeare editions, and handwritten pages by Lincoln and Twain. European and American decorative art are highlighted by Gainsborough's "Blue Boy" and canvases by John Singer Sargent. Outdoors lie 150 acres of gardens.

In nearby Arcadia, the estate of E. J. "Lucky" Baldwin is now the **Arboretum of Los Angeles County** (301 N. Baldwin Ave. 626-821-3222. Adm. fee). It still has the 1885 Victorian cottage built by the aged mining magnate for his 16-year-old bride. The 127 acres of trees and plants include numerous eucalyptus species and one of the nation's great orchid collections.

Photographer at Arboretum of Los Angeles County

Also on the property stand an 1839 adobe house and a lake used as a location in Tarzan movies.

You have a choice of two routes for the remainder of the

drive, both of which end up in the mountains. As the first alternative, head northwest from Pasadena, taking I-210 to Calif. 2, known as the **Angeles Crest Highway** *(Angeles National Forest 626-796-5541. Higher elevations close with first snowfall, Nov.-April).* This road twists eastward for 60 miles through the forested San Gabriel Mountains. Among the peaks—mostly granite and ancient metamorphic rock— you'll find pleasant country for picnicking or hiking. Clear days allow for spectacular views over the L.A. metropolitan area. Also watch for bighorn sheep, black bears, and lots of squawking jays—as well as skiers, since several winter recreation areas operate in season. In **Big Pines,** you're right on top of California's most famous geologic feature, the San Andreas Fault. Past Wrightwood the road descends steeply to Calif. 138, which you follow east to Calif. 18 toward Lake Arrowhead.

Rock Island, Big Bear Lake

The alternate route—required in winter, and quicker and less tortuous if you're not in a mountain-driving mood—has you leaving Pasadena on I-210 E. After merging into I-10, go north on I-215, east on Calif. 30, and then north on Calif. 18.

Either way you'll end up on the **9** **Rim of the World Scenic Byway ★,** heading east toward Big Bear Lake. As you wind along a sheer flank, gaze out over the seemingly endless San Bernardino Valley. For a pleasant side trip, take Calif. 173 to the largely private enclave at **Lake Arrowhead** *(Chamber of Commerce 909-337-3715).* You'd never guess that the lake is man-made. Enjoy the glittering water, edged with white firs and sugar pines, and perhaps take a ride on the paddle wheeler that chugs around it.

Return to Calif. 18 and continue east to the unassuming alpine community of **10** **Big Bear Lake** *(Big Bear Lake Resort Association 909-866-7000 or 800-424-4232),* a headquarters for boating, swimming, mountain biking, hiking, and skiing. If you doubt that southern California has seasons, visit this casual getaway in autumn or winter, and enjoy.

Disneyland and the Beaches

● 60 miles ● 2 days ● Year-round ● On freeways, be prepared for congestion and aggressive drivers.

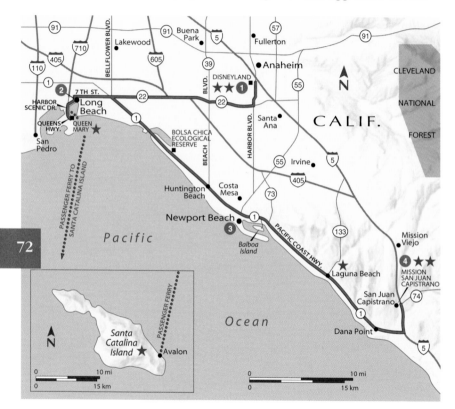

This drive represents pure escape. Leaving the real world behind, it begins at the "Magic Kingdom"—Disneyland. More fantasies line the route in Long Beach at the world's largest ocean liner, on a side trip to the breezy getaway of Santa Catalina Island, and in a string of sun-kissed southern California beach towns, ending at old Mission San Juan Capistrano.

Children and former children alike love ❶ **Disneyland**★★ (*1313 S. Harbor Blvd., Anaheim. 714-781-4565. Adm. fee*), the "Happiest Place on Earth." Opened in 1955 by Walt Disney, its "themed" lands grew out of his own life and imagination. Childhood memories of Missouri at the turn of the century are reflected in the chuffing train and horse-drawn wagons on **Main Street, U.S.A.,** and in the Mark Twain Steamboat in **Frontierland.** Disney's animated films spring into three dimensions in **Fantasyland**

—the Sleeping Beauty Castle, Peter Pan's Flight, Mr. Toad's Wild Ride. In **Adventureland,** storybook exploits come to life on the Jungle Cruise and in the Swiss Family Treehouse. Don't miss the Indiana Jones Adventure in an ancient jungle temple, where perils include erupting lava, creepy mummies with glowing eyes, and . . . well, wait and see.

Sleeping Beauty Castle, Disneyland

Fulfilling Walt's promise that "Disneyland will never be completed as long as there is imagination in the world," **Tomorrowland** features Star Tours, a thrill-a-second motion simulator that takes visitors hurtling through the cosmos. In **New Orleans Square,** the swashbuckling Pirates of the Caribbean and the eerie Haunted Mansion are among the park's most popular attractions. **Mickey's Toontown** tosses you into the wacky world of animation, with bright colors, rubber-walled houses, and a ride on a "Roger Rabbit" taxi.

Next stop: ❷ **Long Beach** *(Convention and Visitors Bureau 562-436-3645 or 800-452-7829).* A popular 19th-century seaside resort, the town's port is the busiest on the West Coast. Among the attractions are the canals winding through the upscale residential area of Naples Island, and art deco buildings on Pine Avenue, downtown.

From downtown, head toward the waterfront, the permanent docking place of the **Queen Mary** ★ *(1126 Queen's Hwy. 562-435-3511. Adm. fee).* At 1,019 feet long, it's the largest luxury passenger vessel afloat, built in 1936. Passengers such as the Duchess of Windsor and Clark Gable may be ghosts now, but their glamorous era comes to life again on a self-guided tour of the ship, whose art deco interior features lavish polished wood, etched glass, and nickel plating. You can see staterooms by taking a guided tour—or by spending the night, because much of the *Queen Mary* has been converted into a hotel.

Alongside the ship and slightly taller than the forward mast is the 200-foot **Megabungee** *(562-435-1880. Wed.-Sun.;*

Disneyland Behind the Scenes

On opening day in 1955, the new park was barely ready. Just before the first guests arrived, staffers were still putting down blacktop. Walt Disney (who hocked his life insurance to finance his dream) didn't have enough cash left to finish landscaping, so he had an employee put Latin name tags on the weeds.

More than 40 years later, Disneyland has become a lush parkland, with a million flowers planted each year. To keep everything looking fresh means collecting 30 tons of trash a day, steam cleaning the park after the guests go home, and brushing on 20,000 gallons of paint annually. Sparkling clean and beaming with optimism, Disneyland keeps the real world at bay.

Disneyland and the Beaches

fee), North America's highest freestanding bungee tower.

Nearby lies a terminal for the 22-mile ferry ride to **Santa Catalina Island ★** *(Catalina Channel Express 310-519-1212 or 800-995-4386. Fare. Chamber of Commerce 310-510-1520. Tours of Avalon and island interior 310-510-2500),* known simply as Catalina Island. You arrive at the only town, **Avalon,** a Mediterranean harbor where yachts bob at anchor and hillside houses are draped in red bougainvillea. The 1929 **Casino Ballroom** *(1 Casino Way. 310-510-7400. Guided tours; adm. fee)* resembles a Moorish fortress in Spain and boasts the world's largest round dance floor, where 3,000 people

Laguna Beach

once swayed to big band sounds. On the ground floor is the **Avalon Theater,** its walls rampant with art deco murals. Downstairs, the **Catalina Island Museum** *(310-510-2414. Adm. fee)* displays Native American artifacts, steamship mementos, and Catalina Island pottery.

Several tour companies offer visitors a glimpse of the unspoiled wilderness of the **island interior ★.** You traverse golden hills above the sea, entering the territory of shaggy bison, originally imported as props for a 1924 Western movie, and wild pigs.

Back on the mainland heading south on the Pacific Coast Highway (Calif. 1), stop at the **Bolsa Chica Ecological Reserve,** just north of Huntington Beach. At this salt marsh, wading egrets and great blue herons are among a hundred other bird species seen annually.

Nicknamed "Surf City, U.S.A.," **Huntington Beach** *(Visitors Bureau 714-969-3492 or 800-729-6232)* inspired Jan and Dean's pop tune of the 1960s. This classic California beach community has 8.5 miles of sandy **beaches ★** with great waves and is home to the U.S. Open of Surfing. The **International Surfing Museum at Huntington Beach** *(411 Olive St. 714-960-3483. Daily June-Sept., Wed.-Sun. rest of year; adm. fee)* celebrates the endless summer with displays showing the evolution of the surfboard and surfing music.

Much of ❸ **Newport Beach** *(Visitors Bureau 949-722-1611 or 800-942-6278),* farther south on Calif. 1, looks as if it just popped new out of the box—urbanly planned, upscale.

74

Epitomizing the mood of California-casual consumption is **Fashion Island** *(Newport Center, off Calif. 1)*, an open-air mall with more than 200 shops and department stores.

On the Balboa Peninsula, you'll find a more down-to-earth California beach community. Each morning at the Newport Pier, the **Dory Fishing Fleet** lands its catch of sand dabs and sculpin; the fish are sold at an open-air market founded around 1890. Along the peninsula are miles of **white sand beaches★**, ending at the Wedge, legendary for bodysurfing. The peninsula shelters the Newport yacht basin and **Balboa Island** *(Via Jamboree Rd. or by ferry from Fun Zone, near Balboa Pavilion; fare for ferry)*, a bit of prime real estate packed with million-dollar cottages. It's fun to look, then browse the shops and have lunch on Marine Avenue.

In **Laguna Beach★** *(Visitors Bureau 949-497-9229)*, art and the outdoors come together like surf and sand. Scalloped coves are edged with palm trees and bird-of-paradise flowers. For another kind of California beauty, the pink **Laguna Art Museum of the Orange County Museum of Art** *(307 Cliff Dr. 949-494-6531. Closed Mon.; adm. fee)* focuses on regional art—appropriate, since Laguna was an early 20th-century hub of the southern California impressionists' plein air movement, which portrayed the effects of outdoor light on such subjects as eucalpytus trees. In July and August during the **Festival of Arts of Laguna Beach** *(949-494-2685 or 800-487-3378. Adm. fee)*, fine artists sell their work, and the open-air **Pageant of the Masters★** *(Adm. fee)* re-creates masterpieces using actors and stage sets. Uncannily realistic, the living works of art range from a van Gogh canvas of wheat harvests to Orpheus carved in a block of Steuben crystal.

Down the coast, you can breathe in the romantic atmosphere of early California at ❹ **Mission San Juan Capistrano★★** *(Calif. 74 at Camino Capistrano, San Juan Capistrano. 949-248-2049. Adm. fee)*, with its adobe walls, sunny gardens, and burbling fountains. Divine mystery seems to pervade the Serra Chapel, where candles glow and profound silence prevails. Built in 1777, this is the only remaining chapel where mission patriarch Junípero Serra said Mass, and is reputedly California's oldest building still in use. The famous swallows return each year on St. Joseph's Day (March 19), celebrated over several days with guitar-playing mariachis and local schoolchildren performing a "swallow dance" (see sidebar this page).

To return to the L.A. area, take I-5 and I-405 N.

Swallows of Capistrano

In 1939 songwriter Leon Rene sat at the breakfast table waiting to eat. It was March 19, and the radio told of tourists thronging an old California mission to see the cliff swallows, which mysteriously returned each year on this date from their winter migration to South America. Rene jokingly called to his wife in the kitchen that before he got his breakfast, he'd probably have to wait till the swallows came back to Capistrano. The rest is musical history. His song, "When the Swallows Come Back to Capistrano," still helps draw crowds to the mission for the big day. In fact, swallow-watchers sometimes outnumber the swallows. Fewer of the birds nest here nowadays, as drought and southern California land development destroy their habitat. However, you might see finches, hummingbirds, doves, crows, blackbirds, kestrels, pigeons, warblers, and other feathered visitors.

75

San Diego Ramble ★

● **415 miles** ● **3 to 5 days** ● **Year-round (although inland areas get hot in summer)** ● **To some highway motorists, "65 mph" seems to be only a suggestion.** ● **Mexican auto insurance required for Tijuana.**

From the beaches and museums of sunny San Diego, this route dips into Mexico, then leads inland. The terrain starts looking parched in Anza-Borrego Desert State Park. Then you pass a desert lake whose surface is more than 200 feet below sea level, and visit Joshua Tree National Park. Next, it's on to the irrigated golf courses and boutiques of the Palm Springs resorts. The road climbs through the San Jacinto Mountains, then drops to the coast, where beach towns are strung like pearls, including chic La Jolla (the jewel).

In 1542 explorer Juan Cabrillo landed at the future site of ❶ **San Diego**★ *(Visitor Center 619-236-1212)*, claiming the region for Spain. Today, the state's second largest city blends a heavenly climate (average temperature 70°F) with the greatest concentration of museums west of the Mississippi, a world-famous zoo, sun-kissed beaches, and well-preserved history.

Start your tour with a stroll through **Old Town San Diego State Historic Park★** *(Off I-5 at Old Town Ave. Visitor Center at Robinson-Rose House. 619-220-5422),* where the clock turns back to the city's Mexican and early American periods. Streets are lined with adobe and wood buildings—haciendas, an 1829 hotel, a stable filled with stagecoaches. Visitors enjoy shopping and dining as mariachis strum guitars. The illusion of the past is especially convincing in the evening, when lights flicker in the old plaza.

If you've never gasped, "I saw a ghost!" you stand a chance at the nearby **Whaley House** *(2482 San Diego Ave. 619-298-2482. Adm. fee),* built in 1856, whose ectoplasmic residents draw great crowds.

East of Old Town, see the way sunlight floods the broad white walls of **Mission Basilica San Diego de Alcalá★** *(10818 San Diego Mission Rd. 619-281-8449. Adm. fee).* Established in 1769 and relocated in 1774, this was the first Spanish mission in California. Founder Padre Junípero Serra's quarters are furnished sparely.

From Old Town head southwest to Point Loma via Calif.

San Diego skyline

209, where **Cabrillo National Monument** *(1800 Cabrillo Memorial Dr. 619-557-5450. Adm. fee)* commemorates mariner Juan Cabrillo, the first European to set foot in California. The Visitor Center has displays on Spanish explorations. Nearby stands the **Old Point Loma Lighthouse** (1855), whose spiral stairway climbs to a remarkably small bedroom. The real reason to visit this point, though, is the view of San Diego Harbor and its huge naval and commercial ships. Gray whales pass by from late December to mid-March.

North of Point Loma, **Mission Bay** is like an outdoor workout spa, with miles of beaches and paths for bikers, in-line skaters, and joggers. It's also the home of Shamu the killer whale, at **Sea World** ★ *(Sea World Dr. exit from I-5. 619-226-3901. Adm. fee).* The park presents performing dolphins, sea lions, otters, and, of course, Shamu doing acrobatic leaps. There are also sharks and an exotic bird show.

Heading toward downtown you reach **Balboa Park** ★ ★ *(Roughly bounded by 6th Ave., Upas St., Florida Dr., and I-5. 619-239-0512),* a 1,200-acre oasis of greenery and culture. Under soaring palms and eucalyptus trees, Spanish "palaces" (built for expositions in 1915 and 1935) house such institutions as the **San Diego Museum of Art** ★ *(619-232-7931. Closed Mon.; adm. fee),* whose collection ranges from baroque Spanish (El Greco) to contemporary California (David Hockney). The focus is on human evolution and anthropology at the **San Diego Museum of Man** *(619-239-2001. Adm. fee),* where see-

ing a mock-up of a Cro-Magnon cave painter is like staring a distant ancestor in the hairy face. The **San Diego Aerospace Museum** *(619-234-8291. Adm. fee)* collects real and reproduction aircraft, including barnstormers and the spy plane *Blackbird.* Other park attractions: the **Timken Museum of Art** *(619-239-5548. Closed Mon.),* full of Russian icons and works by European masters; the **Reuben H. Fleet Space Theater and Science Center** *(619-238-1233. Adm. fee),* complete with IMAX theater and science displays; and several other museums focusing on photography, sports, model railroads, and local history.

Also in Balboa Park you'll find the famous **San Diego Zoo** ★ ★ *(Park Blvd. and Zoo Pl. 619-234-3153. Adm. fee),* featuring more than 4,000 animals, most living in moated enclosures without bars. At the hippos' "African marsh," you peek through an underwater window and dis-

Shamu the killer whale at Sea World, San Diego

cover how agile these bulb-nosed behemoths can be. Among the 800 animal species are rarities seldom seen in zoos, including cuddly koalas from Australia and fierce

Komodo dragons from Indonesia. The zoo is also a botanical garden boasting 6,500 kinds of plants. (Tip: To prevent sore feet, ride the zoo's open-air tram between exhibits.)

In downtown San Diego, have a look at the **Gaslamp Quarter** *(Bounded by 4th and 6th Aves., Broadway, and Harbor Dr.),* where shops and galleries occupy restored Victorian commercial buildings. Then explore the waterfront and the **San Diego Maritime Museum** ★ *(1306 N. Harbor Dr. 619-234-9153. Adm. fee),* home of the 1863 *Star of India,* the oldest iron-hulled sailing ship afloat. The captain's dining table is fitted with wooden strips to stop plates from skittering onto the floor in heaving seas. This nautical museum also includes an 1898 ferryboat and a 1904 luxury steam yacht.

Old Town in Tijuana, Mexico

Zip across Coronado Bridge to the upscale community of **Coronado.** The 1888 landmark **Hotel del Coronado** ★ *(1500 Orange Ave. 619-435-6611)* has a lobby of polished wood with an early Otis birdcage elevator. The hotel's turrets and cupolas inspired neighbor L. Frank Baum in creating the Emerald City of Oz. Movies made here include *Some Like It Hot* with Marilyn Monroe. On the sandbar linking Coronado to the mainland is **Silver Strand State Beach** *(619-435-5184),* popular with families.

Only a dozen miles south of San Diego lies a foreign land—Mexico. A side trip takes you across the border to **Tijuana** ★ *(Baja California Tourism 800-225-2786. Required Mexican auto insurance sold on U.S. side of border).* Having shaken an image of girlie shows and sleaze, a more prosperous Tijuana (tee-HWAH-nah) caters to tourists who throng Avenida Revolución to shop for crafts and sample Mexican food. The **Tijuana Cultural Center** *(Paseo de los Heroes and Ave. Mina, Zona Rio. 011-52-668-41132)* looks at Mexico's archaeology and art. Jai alai, said to be the world's fastest ball game, is played at Palacio Frontón *(7th and Ave. Revolución. 619-231-1910).*

Painted burro, Tijuana

Drive south to **Rosarito** *(Baja California Tourism 800-225-2786),* a sandy playground with resorts and party-hearty bars that serve tropical drinks in coconut shells. The 1920s **Rosarito Beach Hotel** *(31 Benito Juarez Blvd. 011-52-661-20144 or 800-343-8582)* was a hideaway for Hollywood stars.

The trip resumes in San Diego, heading east on I-8 and then north on Calif. 79 through ranchland and up into pine-clad mountains. Stroll the wooden sidewalks of tiny **2 Julian,** an 1870s gold rush town. The **Julian Pioneer**

Hikers at Vulcan Mountain Wilderness Preserve, near Julian

Museum *(760-765-0227. April-Nov. Tues.-Sun., weekends rest of year; adm. fee)* has a bit of everything, from the town's first bathtub to Ulysses S. Grant's china cabinet. Touring the old **Eagle and High Peak Mines** *(Eagle Mining Co., off C St. 619-765-0036. Adm. fee),* you'll see a hard-rock ore tunnel a thousand feet long. While in town, scarf down a big slab of apple pie, a specialty from nearby orchards. Close by, the trails at **Vulcan Mountain Wilderness Preserve** *(Via Farmer Rd. 760-765-2811)* are favorites among hikers.

As rough and dry as your elbow, but considerably more interesting, is **3 Anza-Borrego Desert State Park★** *(760-767-5311),* which sprawls over 900 square miles of busted-up badlands, palm canyons, Native American archaeological sites, spindly ocotillos, and spring wildflowers. To explore the park fully, head east from Julian on Calif. 78, and go north on Route S3 to **Borrego Springs,** where the Visitor Information Center *(west end of Palm Canyon Dr.)* informs you that this "lifeless" desert boasts 60 mammal species, 225 kinds of birds, and 60 species of reptiles and amphibians.

As surprising as a waterfall in the desert is nearby **Palm Canyon** *(Visitor Center 760-767-4205),* which has, well, a waterfall in the desert. It also has a grove of shady fan palms, whose trunks seem to wear Hawaiian grass skirts. Look for desert bighorn sheep.

If you choose to continue eastward on Route S22 (rather than returning to the main route on Calif. 78), you'll be on **Erosion Road,** where signs explain the geological forces that carved this raw land. Detour to **Font's Point,** an overlook onto the painted Borrego Badlands.

If you take Calif. 78 east instead, you reach Ocotillo Wells, where the desert is an open wound. This is the **Ocotillo Wells State Vehicular Recreation Area** *(760-767-5391),* where anyone with a big motor and a tiny brain can drive off-road vehicles across more than 40,000 acres of hills, washes, and dunes.

At the junction with Calif. 86, head north along the ➍ **Salton Sea.** In this dry country, California's largest inland body of water, measuring 35 miles long and up to 15 miles wide, looks like some kind of a mistake—and it was. Around 1905 an irrigation cut allowed flood waters to flow into an ancient seabed that is situated below sea level with no outlet. It's now fed by agricultural runoff. At times as many as four million birds can be found on this sea. Among the 380 species are your everyday ducks and geese, plus endangered brown pelicans and bald eagles. They're protected in the southern section of the **Salton Sea National Wildlife Refuge** *(Visitor Center, 906 W. Sinclair, Calipatria. 760-348-5278).* To fish or go boating at 227 feet below sea level, try the **Salton Sea State Recreation Area** *(North shore, along Calif. 111. Visitor Center, 100-225 State Park Rd. 760-393-3052. Adm. fee).*

Date palms growing by the road into **Indio** *(Chamber of Commerce 760-347-0676)* were introduced from Algeria in 1890 and have made this town the "Date Capital" of the U.S. Along Calif. 111, roadside stands sell every date product you can imagine, and some you can't: Ever tried a date milkshake? In business since 1924, **Shields Date Gardens** *(80-225 Calif. 111. 760-347-0996 or 800-414-2555)* shows a film on the "Romance and Sex Life of the Date."

Newcomers are surprised to learn that a desert isn't just one standard terrain, like a scene in a "Roadrunner" cartoon. You'll find both low Colorado Desert and high Mojave Desert at ➎ **Joshua Tree National Park**★ *(760-367-7511. Adm. fee),* located about 25 miles east of Indio via I-10. Unique on the planet, the Mojave has wild stands of Joshua trees, which are actually giant yuccas. Other park highlights: an Indian oasis, cactus gardens, a cattle rustlers'

Peg Leg Smith Liars' Contest

Around a desert campfire, about 20 people raise their right hands to a night sky as black as a family Bible. They swear to tell lies, all lies, and nothing but lies. After all, this *is* a liars' contest. Most entrants talk about Peg Leg Smith, a mule thief and accomplished barfly who prospected in the 1830s. It's said he struck gold but misplaced his find somewhere among the 600,000 acres of today's Anza-Borrego Desert State Park. Since the 1930s contest audiences have heard all kinds of bald lies—such as how the prospector got a new wooden leg that was too short, and thus he wandered unknowingly in circles. (Contest held at dusk on the Saturday nearest April 1. For details, contact Borrego Springs Chamber of Commerce 760-767-5555.)

81

legendary hideout, and all-around views of desert, mountain, and valley. A sharp-eyed visitor might spy a jackrabbit, sidewinder, bobcat, or golden eagle.

Backtrack to Indio and proceed west on Calif. 111. If you like golf, welcome to paradise. You're passing through the

Joshua Tree National Park

Coachella Valley, which has 90 courses with 1,526 holes. (Not to mention 30,000 swimming pools.) It's easy to forget you're in the Colorado Desert. To learn about the desert, pause at the 1,200-acre **Living Desert Wildlife and Botanical Park** *(47-900 Portola Ave. 760-346-5694. Adm. fee),* in the town of **Palm Desert.** Animals range from local mountain lions and bighorn sheep to African birds and speedy cheetahs (whose claws, you learn, work like cleats on a track shoe). Gardens showcase North American desert plants.

Cradled between the San Jacinto and Little San Bernardino Mountains, ❻ **Palm Springs** ★ *(Visitors Bureau 760-770-9000 or 800-417-3529)* first boomed in the 1930s as Hollywood stars discovered this desert retreat. Sunshine, fashionable shopping, fine restaurants, and golf resorts are among the draws.

More than 2,000 years ago, the Agua Caliente band of Cahuilla Indians (who still own close to 23,000 acres around Palm Springs) settled near the mineral springs of the **Indian Canyons** ★ *(End of S. Palm Canyon Dr. 760-325-1053. Sept.-*

June; adm. fee). On a network of trails you visit an oasis of 3,000 fan palms in Palm Canyon, view tribal rock art in lush Andreas Canyon, and perhaps see wild ponies in more remote Murray Canyon.

Nearby is an enterprise that began when old-time character actor "Cactus Slim" Moorten married a research botanist in 1938—**Moorten Botanical Garden** *(1701 S. Palm Canyon Dr. 760-327-6555. Adm. fee)*. At this homey spot, more than 3,000 desert plant varieties create an almost surreal world where cactuses may grow bulbous like beach balls or hairy like grandpa's beard.

In downtown Palm Springs, past is present at the **Village Green Heritage Center** *(221 S. Palm Canyon Dr. 760-323-8297. Mid-Oct.–May closed Mon.-Tues.; adm. fee)*, a collection of historic building museums. Here the **McCallum Adobe,** built in 1884 by the region's first white settler, displays Cahuilla Indian artifacts and photos of movie celebrities vacationing in the desert. **Miss Cornelia's Little House** (1893) belonged to the city's first hotel keeper; it now displays regional artifacts. And the main product at **Ruddy's 1930s General Store Museum** *(760-327-2156. Thurs.-Sun. Oct.-June, weekends only July-Sept.)* is nostalgia. Shelves hold patent medicines and beauty aids. It's remarkable how long some brand names—Tootsie Roll and Camel cigarettes, to name a couple—have lasted.

A balance of art and nature characterizes the **Palm Springs Desert Museum** ★ *(101 Museum Dr. 760-325-7186. Closed Mon.; adm. fee)*. On one hand you'll see animal dioramas and a Coachella Valley mural; on the other are California landscape paintings by James Swinnerton and others.

To get the big picture of the Coachella Valley from the north end of town, ride the **Palm Springs Aerial Tramway** ★★ *(Off Calif. 111 at Tramway Rd. 760-325-1391. Adm. fee)* up Mount San Jacinto. Ascending more than a vertical mile along a rocky scarp, you'll witness a change of landscapes equal to that between Sonora, Mexico, and the Arctic Circle, as the temperature drops 35 to 40 degrees. You arrive at a 13,000-acre wilderness with 54 miles of trails; on a clear day there's a 75-mile view. The mountain station serves meals.

Continue on Calif. 111, then take I-10 W to Banning, where you pick up the **Palms to Pines Highway** (Calif. 243). This scenic byway climbs from the desert into chapar-

83

Date palm near Indio

ral and oak woodlands, passes the amusingly named Lake Fulmor, and winds through the San Jacinto Mountains to **7** **Idyllwild** (*Tourist Information 951-659-3259*), a resort community near Tahquitz Peak (8,823 feet).

Zigzag south and west on Calif. 74, 371, 79, and 76 through low, hilly ranch country. Stop in at the **8** **Palomar Observatory** (*N on Rte. S6. 760-742-2119*), home of the 200-inch Hale telescope, which visitors can look at (but not through). Housed under a 13-story white dome, it can

Mission San Luis Rey de Francia

peer at celestial objects one billion light-years away.

Proceed west along Calif. 76 to the small **Mission San Antonio de Pala** (*760-742-3317. Museum closed Mon.; adm. fee*), built in 1816 as a branch of Mission San Luis Rey de Francía. The only original mission chapel where an Indian congregation still worships, it displays restored murals, the original altar, and minerals and semiprecious stones. At **9** **Mission San Luis Rey de Francía** (*4050 Mission Ave., San Luis Rey. 760-757-3651. Adm. fee*), the 1798 mission church has a polychrome altar and a Madonna Chapel aglow with votive candles and warm with their waxy scent. The cloister museum displays silk vestments and Luiseño Indian baskets.

When you reach the ocean, turn south on I-5. In **Encinitas** the **Self-Realization Fellowship Retreat and Hermitage** (*215 K St. 760-753-1811. Closed Mon.*) was founded in 1937 by Paramahansa Yogananda, who brought Indian meditation techniques to the West and wrote *Autobiography of a Yogi*. Ponds and gardens rest on the bluff above a surfing beach that locals call "Swami's."

South of Del Mar, **10** **Torrey Pines State Reserve**★ (*N. Torrey Pines Rd. 858-755-2063. Parking fee*) preserves its namesake trees—ice age survivors that grow natively only here and on Santa Rosa Island. Keep driving south

84

on Torrey Pines Road, where you're likely to see hang gliders soaring like paper kites. If you're the type, ask the way to nearby clothing-optional **Black's Beach.**

Proceed south on Torrey Pines Road to the **Birch Aquarium at Scripps** *(Expedition Way. 858-534-3474. Adm. fee),* which looks at sea life in both the North and South Pacific. A kelp forest sways in a 50,000-gallon tank, where a 5-foot sea bass looks like a blimp beside the yellowtails.

Torrey Pines Road leads to elegant **La Jolla** (la HOY-a) *(Tourist Information 858-454-1444).* Perched on sandstone bluffs above the sea, the town has a Mediterranean look that evokes coastal Italy. Art galleries and upscale restaurants abound. So do surfers, with no visible means of support except the waves; check 'em out at **Windansea Beach,** at the foot of Palomar Street. **La Jolla Cove** *(Along Ocean Blvd.)* is popular with tide poolers and snorkelers. Inside La Jolla Cave and Shell Shop *(1325 Coast Blvd. 858-454-6080),* a tunnel

Cliffs at Torrey Pines State Reserve

descends to **Sunny Jim Cave** *(Adm. fee),* a grotto where surf surges in. Downtown, the **Museum of Contemporary Art, San Diego** *(700 Prospect St. 858-454-3541. Closed Mon.; adm. fee)* is devoted to minimalist, conceptual, and pop works of art.

From La Jolla, rejoin I-5 S for the return to San Diego.

Great Parks ★★

● 610 miles, plus side trips ● 5 to 7 days ● Mid-spring through mid-autumn ● In winter, Tioga Road closes across Yosemite National Park. In summer, the visitor population of Yosemite rises dramatically, as does the thermometer in Death Valley.

This loop from Fresno around the southern Sierra Nevada mountains roams through a world of wonders, beginning with Yosemite and its sublime granite walls, alpine meadows, and rainbow-misted waterfalls. After a stop at North America's oldest lake, there's a side trip to Bodie, the West's biggest (and once baddest) ghost town. The drive heads down the eastern scarp of the mountains to the recreation lands around Mammoth Lakes and Mount Whitney. A side trip to Death Valley explores an immensity of grit and blue skies. Finally, it visits the towering forests and uplifting backcountry of Sequoia and Kings Canyon National Parks.

The butt of countless jokes on late-night television shows, the monumentally nondescript agricultural city of **1 Fresno** *(Visitors Bureau 559-233-0836 or 800-788-0836)* is the gateway to Yosemite. But before you head for the exit, see the **Fresno Metropolitan Museum of History, Science, and Art** *(1555 Van Ness Ave. 559-441-1444. Closed Mon.; adm. fee),* which has an interesting exhibit on native son and author William Saroyan. Also pop into the more contemporary **Fresno Art Museum** *(2233 N. 1st St. 559-441-4220. Closed Mon.; adm. fee),* focused on American, Mexican, and Peruvian art. The city's finest Victorian house, the **Meux Home Museum** *(Tulare and R Sts. 559-233-8007. Fri.-Sun.; adm. fee),* was built with towers and gables in 1889 by a Civil War doctor. About 7 miles west of downtown, California's "raisin king," Theodore Kearney, built the 1903 French Renaissance château now restored as the **M. Theodore Kearney Mansion Museum** *(7160 W. Kearney Blvd. 559-441-0862. Fri.-Sun.; adm. fee),* with art nouveau and Victorian furnishings.

Wildflowers, Yosemite Valley

Head north on Calif. 41 to the south entrance of one of the world's natural shrines, **2 Yosemite National Park ★ ★** *(209-372-0200. Adm. fee).* Named for the Native Americans who once inhabited the valley, Yosemite encompasses almost 1,200 square miles of the Sierra Nevada. Visit **Mariposa Grove ★** *(Mid-May–mid-Oct.; fee for tram),* whose giant sequoias may live for nearly 3,000 years and weigh two million pounds. Biggest, and oldest at 2,700 years, is the Grizzly Giant, so lofty that lightning struck it six times during one storm.

Ahead on Wawona Road *(Calif. 41)* are the historic cabins and covered bridge (1875) of the **Pioneer Yosemite History Center.** Farther ahead, turn onto Glacier Point Road *(closed in winter),* which climbs through red firs and lodgepole pines to one of the park's—and America's—most exhilarating, profound vistas, **Glacier Point ★ ★.** Before you unfolds a view that makes your knees wobbly: High Sierra peaks in levitation beyond an airy chasm, granite Half Dome, and the Yosemite Valley down a 3,200-foot cliff. Arrive early and find a quiet spot.

Back on Wawona Road, emerge from the Wawona Tunnel to a timeless view of **Yosemite Valley ★ ★** from El

Capitan to Cloud's Rest. Just ahead is **Bridalveil Fall,** which drops 620 feet from a "hanging valley," a testament to the power of plate tectonics, glaciers, and running water.

Continue straight on one-way Southside Drive past Sentinel Rock to the heart of the park and **Curry Village** *(Lodging reservations 559-252-4848).* Road access continues to Pines Campground and Yosemite Valley Stables, while a hiking trail leads to postcard-perfect **Vernal** and **Nevada Falls★.** On ahead is the trail to much-photographed **Mirror Lake and Meadow.** (One tip: To capture the lake reflecting nearby cliffs, go on a windless early morning or moonlit evening. The lake has water only in spring and early summer.) Nearby looms **Half Dome★ ★,** a thundering mass of granite; its summit soars 4,748 feet above the valley.

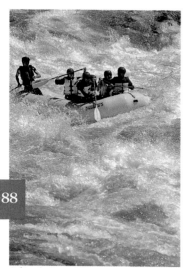
Rafting the Merced River, just outside Yosemite

Looping west on Northside Drive, pause to learn about natural and human history at the **Valley Visitor Center** in Yosemite Village. Also peek into the nearby **Ahwahnee Hotel★** *(559-252-4848),* a classic 1927 lodge whose rustic design incorporates 5,000 tons of stone. The dining room has floor-to-ceiling windows and log pillars.

Drive on and spend some quality time at one of the world's highest cascades, **Yosemite Falls★ ★** *(Via short trail),* which tumbles 2,425 feet down three drops. Farther ahead, forces of nature have eroded away most of the surrounding terrain, leaving the seemingly unbroken granite surface of **El Capitan.** Sweeping 3,245 feet above its base, this is one of the largest exposed monoliths on earth. (Those tiny specks moving slowly are climbers.)

Bear right on Big Oak Flat Road to Crane Flat, where you turn right on the Tioga Road *(closed in winter).* After a half mile, you can make a side trip to the **Tuolumne Grove of Big Trees,** where a pedestrian-only road passes among impressive giant sequoias and through Yosemite's last walk-through tree trunk.

Proceed up Tioga Road toward Yosemite's high country. After 14 miles the mixed evergreen forest begins to thin. At **Olmsted Point★** walk the quarter-mile trail to a spectacular viewpoint down to Half Dome and up to Tenaya Lake. Under a thin blue sky at 8,575 feet lies **Tuolumne Meadows★ ★,** where the Tuolumne River flows among wildflowers in midsummer. You'll find a Visitor Center and access to trails (including the John Muir and Pacific Crest trails).

Leave the park via **Tioga Pass** (9,945 feet), the highest automobile pass in California. Once past glacial **Ellery Lake** the road begins a tortuous descent of the eastern flank of the Sierra Nevada through **Lee Vining Canyon** (Beware of sheer drops and a distinct lack of guardrails).

On reaching US 395 at Lee Vining, detour a mile north to 730,000-year-old **Mono Lake**★ *(Visitor Center 760-647-3044. Daily May-Oct., call for off-season schedule),* where towers of white tufa (calcium carbonate) rise from startlingly blue water. Although Mark Twain called it the "Dead Sea of the West," Mono Lake's alkaline water supports alkali flies and four trillion brine shrimp that help lure 98 species of waterbirds, including 60,000 California gulls *(March-Aug.).* October brings some 800,000 eared grebes, so many that they look like pepper sprinkled on the lake.

Bridalveil Fall, Yosemite National Park

Near the southern shore stands 600-year-old **Panum Crater,** one of 21 volcanic cones that make up the continent's youngest mountain range. For a rare contrast, look up from this sagebrush desert to the perennial snows of the Sierra Nevada.

A side trip now takes you to the largest unrestored

ghost town in the West, at **3** **Bodie State Historic Park**★ ★ *(18 miles N via US 395, then 13 miles E on Calif. 270; the last 3 miles are unpaved and difficult in muddy conditions, and may be closed by snow in winter. 760-647-6445. Adm. fee).* Here the Methodist church, houses, livery stable, and 170 other buildings look as if people just wandered away, leaving pots on the stoves and aces on the gambling hall tables. In fact Bodie folded its hand more than 50 years ago. In 1880 this gold boomtown boasted 10,000 people, 30 mining companies, 65 watering holes, and a well-deserved reputation for violence. A little girl on her way there wrote a famous diary entry: "Goodbye God, I'm going to Bodie." In the Miners' Union Hall, a museum displays mining equipment and household belongings.

Heading south on US 395, consider a 15-mile detour

Tufa formations, Mono Lake

along the **June Lake Loop** *(Also known as Calif. 158; 4 miles S of Lee Vining. Call Mono Basin Scenic Area Visitor Center 760-647-3044. Northern portion of road closed in winter).* On this scenic drive, you'll visit four lakes set amid raw, rocky mountains, softened in late September by the gold of aspens. **Oh! Ridge** is named for its outstanding view of June Lake and Carson Peak (10,909 feet). The road leading to the Oh! Ridge Campground winds to June Lake's sandy swimming beach.

Driving south on US 395, you're surrounded by **Inyo**

National Forest (*Call Mono Basin Scenic Area Visitor Center 760-647-3044*), enjoyed by all kinds of outdoor enthusiasts. Hikers traipse along trails frequented by bear and mule deer, while fishermen try their luck in the region's trout-filled lakes. Boating and camping are also popular.

One of the forest's busiest sections is the Mammoth Lakes area, the heart of which is ❹ **Mammoth Lakes**★ (*Turn off at Calif. 203. Visitors Bureau 760-934-8006 or 888-466-2666*). A bustling town, Mammoth Lakes is also the name for the surrounding region of mountains and small glacial lakes. The dormant volcano **Mammoth Mountain**★ (11,053 feet) is a popular ski resort and summer mountain-biking hub. For a god's-eye view, ride up in the **gondola** (*760-934-2571. Adm. fee*).

A top area attraction is 798-acre **Devils Postpile National Monument**★ (*760-934-2289. June-Oct. Shuttle bus mandatory; fare*), where 60-foot-high columns of basalt appear to have been driven like pilings

Mule deer

into the ground. Actually, they resulted when extruded lava flows cooled, then cracked. A short hike leads to the top, where you see what one ranger calls "nature's tile floor," created about 10,000 years ago when a glacier cleanly sheared off the column tops.

Continuing south on US 395, cross over the 7,000-foot Sherwin Summit, all rocks and evergreens. Then at Bishop, detour to the **Laws Railroad Museum and Historical Site** (*4.5 miles N on US 6, then 0.5 mile on Silver Canyon Rd. 760-873-5950*) to see the *Slim Princess* steam locomotive, vintage railroad cars, 1883 depot museum, and exhibit-filled historic buildings on 11 acres.

Out of Big Pine, make a side trip to the ❺ **Ancient Bristlecone Pine Forest**★★ (*12 miles via Calif. 168 and 8 miles on White Mountain Rd. 760-873-2573. Paved to Schulman Grove. No gas, water, or services*). Here, above 10,000 feet in the White Mountains, grow the world's most ancient trees, bristlecone pines (*Pinus longaeva*). Meeting a 4,000-year-old tree has an undeniable emotional impact. Here is an elder of the earth, bent by time and polished by wind, ice, and sand. Yet on a summer day the tree exudes youthful life, as surely as its bristled cones drip scented resin. At Schulman Grove, a **Visitor Center** (*Daily mid-*

Manzanar National Historic Site

Shorty Harris

92

Beloved Death Valley prospector Frank "Shorty" Harris discovered the Bullfrog gold mine, whose riches lured three railroads across the desert and in 1905 built the now ghost town of Rhyolite, Nevada. Shorty himself never reaped much of the rewards from his big find. The few claims he had, he sold for a fraction of their worth, and he spent most of his time prospecting the valley for other strikes. Yet Shorty—he stood about as tall as his burro—was hardly the miserly sort. When he had money, he spent it lavishly on himself and his friends.

June–Sept., weekends early June and Oct.) has exhibits on the pines and tree rings, plus an interpretive trail. A 4.5-mile trail loops through Methuselah Grove, home of the **Methuselah Tree,** which has been growing for 4,723 years. Bow your head: This is the oldest tree on earth, growing here when pharaohs ruled ancient Egypt.

Take US 395 south to **Independence** and the **Eastern California Museum** *(155 Grant. St. 760-878-0258. Closed Tues.).* Artifacts from nearby Manzanar, the World War II relocation center, include a model train fashioned from tin cans and other items made by internees. Also on exhibit are Paiute and Shoshone baskets and beadwork.

Five miles south lies the **Manzanar National Historic Site.** You can't make out much of the relocation camp, which housed 10,000 Japanese-Americans shamefully interred by the U.S. government along with Japanese aliens from 1942 to 1945. Just a few foundations and two stone guardhouses with pagoda roofs remain, but its desolation provokes thought.

When you reach Lone Pine, turn right at the town's only traffic light onto Whitney Portal Road *(closed mid-Nov.–April).* On this side trip you'll pass through the **Alabama Hills,** a movie and television location where the ghost of Hopalong Cassidy still chases bandits hiding behind the rocks. Ahead are the camping, picnic, and fishing areas of **Whitney Portal.** This is the base of **Mount Whitney★** *(Lone Pine Ranger Station 760-876-6200. Day and overnight hikes by permit only, late May–mid-Oct.; reservations highly recommended; call 888-374-3773).* The summit, at 14,494 feet the highest real estate in the lower 48 states, can be reached by a very strenuous 11-mile climb at the end of Whitney Portal Road (8,367 feet); allow two to three days.

It's a quirk of nature that the most elevated point in the contiguous United States is situated so close to the lowest. You can "bottom out" on a side trip to ❻ **Death Valley National Park★★** *(760-786-2331. Adm. fee).* From Lone Pine take Calif. 136 past the Owens Lake Bed, which went dry after Los Angeles shunted Owens Valley streams into its aqueduct in 1913. Pick up Calif. 190, crossing through the Panamint Range into Death Valley. This stripped-down kingdom of bent mountains, hammering heat, and big lonesomeness got its name in 1849 from pioneers desperately glad to be leaving. The basin's record temperature is 134°F, exceeded only in the Sahara, and the desert sands may reach 200°F. The average rainfall here is only 1.71 inches a year.

Just past Stovepipe Wells are 14 square miles of sand dunes, a "lifeless" desert where kangaroo rats eat mesquite seeds and coyotes roam. At the junction where Calif. 190 turns south, you can turn north for 35 miles to **Scotty's Castle★** *(760-786-2392. Food and gas available. Adm. fee),* a complex of 1920s buildings in Spanish style, built with the deep pockets of a Chicago businessman and the grandiose dreams of a charming hustler known as Death Valley Scotty. Nearby is 500-foot-deep **Ubehebe Crater,** caused by a volcanic steam explosion.

Go south on Calif. 190 to **Furnace Creek,** where natural springs create a welcome oasis of date palms and even a golf course. This is a hub of visitor facilities and accommodations such as the elegant 1927 **Furnace Creek Inn** *(760-786-2345),* whose swimming pool is fed by thermal water at 84°F. The **Borax Museum** *(Furnace Creek Ranch)* shows wagons and a 1914 steam train from the Death Valley Railroad.

Badwater Road leads south to the **Devil's Golf Course,** a jumble of crystal blocks that are 95 percent pure table salt. Ahead is the salty pool called **Badwater★** at 279.8 feet below sea level. The Western Hemisphere's low point lies a few miles west, at 282 feet below sea level. As you return north, detour on **Artist's Drive ★,** named for its palette of reds and yellows (iron oxides), greens and violets (volcanic minerals). Continue north to

Afternoon storm, Death Valley National Park

Calif. 190 and turn southeast to **Zabriskie Point,** a lookout over ancient lake beds tilted into weird badlands. Continue to **Dante's View★,** where the classic scenery of Death Valley sweeps from salt flats up to the 11,049-foot summit of Telescope Peak.

Leave Death Valley on Calif. 190 west. At US 395 head south through rocks and scrub to Calif. 14, which you take to Calif. 178. Go west alongside the South Fork Kern River to ❼ **Isabella Lake** *(760-379-5646),* a popular fishing spot for trout, bass, and catfish.

Take Calif. 155 west to Calif. 65, then head north until you reach Calif. 198. Go east to **Sequoia** and **Kings Canyon National Parks**★ *(559-565-3341. Adm. fees),* which cover an area the size of Rhode Island. The parks preserve a swath of the southern Sierra Nevada, a 400-mile-long mountain range that is basically one gigantic uplifted block, mostly granite. During the last ice age, it was sculptured by the grinding passage of glaciers into U-shaped canyons, sawtooth ridges, and lakes. Here on the western flank grow giant sequoias, the largest living things on earth.

After entering ⑧ **Sequoia National Park** on the Generals Highway, stop for information at the **Foothills Visitor Center** *(559-565-3341. Obtain tickets for Crystal Cave*

Horse packing through Granite Basin, Kings Canyon National Park

if you plan to visit; fee for cave). Then zigzag up through rugged foothills of chaparral and oak, keeping an eye out for the **Hospital Rock** picnic area, where there are bedrock mortars and pictographs (probably made for religious purposes) left on an overhanging rock by ancient Yokuts; the rock got its name because early settlers with illnesses or broken bones would rest here in its shelter.

Ahead, Crystal Cave Road leads to **Crystal Cave** *(Daily mid-June–Labor Day; Fri.-Mon. May, early June, and Sept.*

Obtain advance tickets at Foothills Visitor Center; adm. fee).
Stone formations resemble curtains, a rank of organ
pipes, and other curious creations of cavedom. Drive on,
perhaps taking the side road *(turn off at Giant Forest Village;
closed in winter)* to **Crescent Meadow,** where spring wildflowers grow in a marshy clearing amid giant sequoias. You
pass granite **Moro Rock,** where steps lead to a spectacular view of the southern Sierra Nevada.

As you travel through the **Giant Forest★★,**
stop at the **General Sherman Tree★★,** in volume
the world's biggest living thing—274.9 feet tall and
102.5 feet around, with a trunk weighing about 2.8
million pounds. Nearby, the **Congress Trail** loops
past giant sequoias that writer-naturalist John Muir
described as "heaving their massive crowns into the
sky from every ridge and slope."

Generals Highway leads on to **Kings Canyon
National Park** *(559-335-2856 or 209-565-3341. Road
closed in winter past Hume Lake),* where you turn
north onto Calif. 180. Stop for park information at
the **Grant Grove Visitor Center.** In the hushed
cathedral of **Grant Grove★** stands the world's
third largest tree, a rust-colored archbishop about
2,000 years old.

Towering sequoias, Sequoia National Park

Ahead, you leave the park for a while. Past the side
road to **Hume Lake,** stop at **Junction Overlook★,** where
rough peaks frame the confluence of the South and Middle
Forks of the Kings River. This is one of North America's
deepest gorges, making a 7,800-foot rise from the river to
the top of Spanish Mountain—greater than Arizona's Grand
Canyon. Tours are offered at **Boyden Cavern** *(209-736-
2708. May-Oct.; adm. fee),* which features your typical cave
items, such as stalactites and stalagmites.

After re-entering the national park, the stream-carved V-
shaped canyon changes to a magnificent U-shaped valley,
created by moving, debris-laden glaciers that cut through
during the ice age like immense rasps. Shaggy incense
cedars give their name to **Cedar Grove,** a hiking hub. Consider a stop at **Zumwalt Meadow** where a nature trail leads
to a view of the Kings River, marshes, and granite monoliths.
At **Road's End,** trails wander into the pristine backcountry
that makes up more than 85 percent of the park.

To finish the drive, take Calif. 180 back downhill and
continue west to Fresno.

Mother Lode and

● **444 miles** ● **4 to 6 days** ● **Spring through fall**
● **Summer brings heavy traffic, especially at Lake
Tahoe** ● **Calif. 4 beyond Bear Valley closed in winter.**

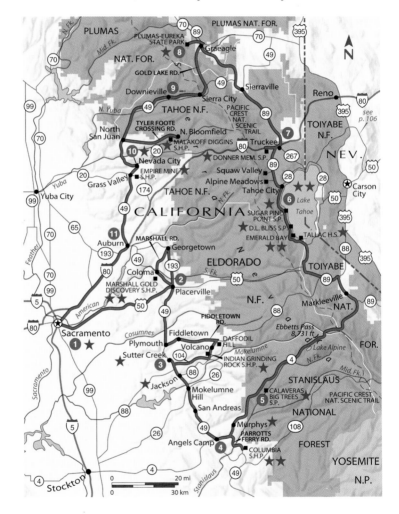

see p. 106

Some of California's prettiest countryside lies along the western slope of the Sierra Nevada. Today, it's a peaceful region of rolling hills and little towns. But around 150 years ago, the air exploded with the shouts of miners and the ringing of their picks on rocky ground. During the California Gold Rush, thousands of fortune seekers swarmed into the Mother Lode, and every little valley seemed to have its overnight boomtown. Many a Hang-town or Pokerville began as a cluster of tents that sheltered stores and, of course, saloons—often just two whiskey barrels with a board laid on top. Some boom-towns went bust; others grew into permanent settlements. You'll see both on this loop drive. It begins in Sacramento, takes in most of the Mother Lode, and also visits picturesque Lake Tahoe, a liquid sapphire set among emerald mountains.

Gold nuggets from the Sierra Nevada

❶ **Sacramento**★ *(Visitors Bureau 916-264-7777)* supplied forty-niners heading to the gold fields—not a bad business, when a merchant could get a dollar for a potato and 50 dollars for a shovel. The growing town became the western terminus of the Pony Express and the transcontinental railroad, as well as the state capital.

Start by exploring the **Old Sacramento State Historic Park**★ *(Bet. I-5 and the Sacramento River, from I St. to Capitol Ave. Visitor Center, 2nd and K Sts. 916-442-7644).* As you clomp on wooden sidewalks in front of 19th-century buildings (now shops, restaurants, and museums), you get a nice feeling of days when this riverside district was the

city's shipping and commercial center. The most significant structure is the brick **B.F. Hastings Building** *(2nd and J Sts.),* containing the state's 1854 supreme court chambers and exhibits on the Pony Express and Wells Fargo.

While in Old Sac, don't miss the vast **California State Railroad Museum**★★ *(2nd and I Sts. 916-552-5252 ext. 7245. Adm. fee).*

Along Front Street, Old Sacramento

Among its treasures are a gleaming 1862 locomotive, a private rail car with stained-glass windows and fireplace, a post office car where mail was sorted en route, and a 1929 sleeping car that seems to rock and sway along the tracks while a town's lights whisk by outside. Steam train excursions *(April-Sept.; fare)* leave the Central Pacific Freight Depot at Front and K Streets.

Bringing you back to the present, the nearby **Discovery Museum** *(101 I St. 916-264-7057. Closed Mon.; adm. fee)* looks

Mother Lode and the Sierra

at science and technology, and traces local people from Native Americans to Victorians to computer makers. A few blocks south, California's oldest public art museum (1885)— the **Crocker Art Museum** *(3rd and O Sts. 916-264-5423. Closed Mon.; adm. fee)*—is housed in an Italianate Victorian mansion rich with woodwork and plaster moldings. Its exhibits include 19th- and 20th-century California art.

To see every model that Ford built from 1903 to 1953 (and more), go about a mile south of Old Sac via Front

Hangtown's Gold Bug Mine, Placerville

Street to the **Towe Ford Museum** *(2200 Front St. 916-442-6802. Adm. fee)*.

About 10 blocks east of the Sacramento River, the **California State Capitol** *(10th St. bet. L and N Sts. 916-324-0333)* has an elaborate rotunda with molded plasterwork and a lofty 120-foot dome. In one wing, early 20th-century offices have been restored. A bit north, the **Governor's Mansion State Historic Park** *(1526 H St. 916-323-3047.*

Guided tours; adm. fee) is the Second Empire Italianate mansion where California governors lived from 1903 to 1968, ending with Ronald Reagan.

In 1839 larger-than-life Swiss immigrant John Sutter built Sacramento's first settlement, east of today's downtown at **Sutter's Fort State Historic Park** ★ *(2701 L St. 916-445-4422. Adm. fee)*. His adobe fort became an important hub for travelers and traders during an era that comes to life in the original main building and reconstructed residences and shops. At the adjacent **California State Indian Museum** ★ *(2618 K St. 916-324-0971. Adm. fee)*, exhibits range from a one-log canoe to fine ceremonial dance costumes.

Now it's off to the gold country! Take US 50 east to mostly modern ❷ **Placerville** *(Visitors Bureau 530-621-5885)*, where **Hangtown's Gold Bug Park** *(2501 Bedford Ave. 530-642-5232)* boasts the nation's only city-owned gold mine *(daily April-Oct., weekends rest of year; adm. fee)*. The wheeled relics at **El Dorado County Historical Museum** *(El Dorado County Fairgrounds, 104 Placerville Dr. 530-621-5865. Wed.-Sun.; donation)* include a Concord stagecoach.

A side trip jogs northwest on Calif. 49 (as in forty-niners) to **Coloma,** site of **Marshall Gold Discovery State Historic Park** ★ ★ *(530-622-3470. Adm. fee)*. Here the California Gold

98

Rush began in 1848, when James Marshall saw small flakes in the tailrace of John Sutter's mill. He shared the big news with his partner and a couple of employees . . . and the word soon spread. Enjoy the now peaceful valley of the American River, with its oak-studded hills and painterly light. There's a museum with Native American artifacts and Marshall's pocket watch, but the best exhibits are outdoors— Marshall's cabin and a reproduction of the mill, plus a Chinese store, church, and other buildings of old Coloma.

Follow Marshall Road northeast to **Georgetown,** whose Main Street shows off the 1850s Wells Fargo building and Odd Fellows Hall.

Take Calif. 193 south to Placerville again. Then get on Calif. 49 south, passing through ranch country to Plymouth. From here, take Fiddletown Road east to **Fiddletown,** an unspoiled hamlet with a community hall that was once a stagecoach stop. An 1850s Chinese herbal doctor's shop, the **Chew Kee Store Museum** *(14357 Littletown Rd. April-Oct. Sat.)* displays remedies, gambling devices, and a shrine.

Continue on Fiddletown Road, turning right on Shake

Sierra Nevada foothills, near Coloma

Ridge Road. At the junction with Ram's Horn Grade lies **Daffodil Hill,** which goes bloomin' crazy with 300,000 daffodils in mid-March through mid-April. Now take Ram's Horn Grade to **Volcano,** a pleasantly uncommercial village with an 1863 brick hotel. Continue on Pine Grove-

Black Bart

In the 1870s, the gentle-man bandit robbed 28 Wells Fargo stagecoaches of their gold, never stealing from the passengers. His shotgun unloaded, his face was hidden under a flour sack cut with eye holes. And he always left a scrap of poetry signed "Black Bart, the Po8."

Black Bart made the mistake of dropping a handkerchief during his 29th robbery. Its laundry mark was traced to San Francisco, and in 1883 he was cap-tured. In reality Black Bart was prominent busi-nessman Charles Bolton. After serving 6 years in the pen, the courtly bandit was released. It's said Wells Fargo put him on pension on the condition he would not resume his banditry.

Western storefront at Columbia S.H.P.

Volcano Road to the oak-studded meadows of **Indian Grinding Rock State Historic Park** ★ *(209-296-7488. Adm. fee)*, named for an immense limestone slab with more than 1,100 mortar holes where Miwok Indians pul-verized acorns; a museum presents regional Native Ameri-can artifacts and structures.

Take Ridge Road (Calif. 104) west to Calif. 49, then jog north to ❸ **Sutter Creek** ★, whose charming main street is lined with brick, wood, and stone buildings of gold rush days. The 1873 **Knight Foundry** *(81 Eureka St. Closed to the public)* was the last working water-powered foundry and machine shop in the United States. Plaques explain its historical significance.

Head south again on Calif. 49. As you descend a hill into Jackson, look left for the headframe of the **Kennedy Mine** (1856), once North America's deepest mine at 5,912 feet. From here you have a great view of **Jackson** ★, site of the 58-foot-high **Kennedy Tailing Wheels** *(Jackson Gate Rd.)*, which lifted and moved mining debris. See large working models of mine operations at the **Amador County Museum** *(225 Church St. 209-223-6386. Wed.-Sun.; donation)*, along with an 1859 house and a narrow-gauge locomotive reproduc-tion. Other sights include the 1894 **St. Sava Serbian Ortho-dox Church** *(724 N. Main St.)*, with its terraced cemetery; and the 1862 **National Hotel** *(2 Water St.)*, still a social center.

Ahead lies **Mokelumne Hill,** a placer-gold mining town where miners fought violently over claims so packed with ore they were limited to 16 square feet. The 1874 **Hotel Leger** *(8304 Main St.)* has a wraparound balcony.

A few miles south in **San Andreas,** gentleman bandit Black Bart (see sidebar this page) was a guest in the hoosegow after a stagecoach robbery in 1883. See his jail cell and the courtroom where he was tried at the **Calaveras County Museum** *(30 N. Main St. 209-754-6579. Adm. fee)*; there are also Miwok and pioneer relics.

Continue south to ❹ **Angels Camp** *(Visitor Center 209-736-0049 or 800-225-3764)*. The surface gold had played out here when a man's muzzle loader jammed and he fired it into the ground—revealing gold-bearing quartz that launched a hard-rock mining boom. Main Street is lined with iron-shuttered buildings, many with overhang-ing balconies. Tip your hat to the **Angels Hotel** *(1287 S. Main St.)*, where in 1865 Mark Twain reportedly heard the yarn he would pen as "The Celebrated Jumping Frog of

Calaveras County," making him famous. Travelers can enter their own acrobatic amphibians in the annual Jumping Frog Jubilee *(third weekend in May)*. The **Angels Camp Museum** *(753 S. Main St. 209-736-2963. Adm. fee)* displays everything from a square piano to a hearse.

Leave town east on Calif. 4. Take a side trip south on Parrotts Ferry Road, stopping first at **Moaning Cavern** *(209-736-2708. Adm. fee)*, discovered by miners in 1851. To explore the multihued limestone cave, you make a dizzying descent on a spiral stairway or rappel down a 180-foot rope (no experience required).

Camping in Desolation Wilderness, off Calif. 89

Farther south on Parrotts Ferry Road lies **Columbia State Historic Park** ★★ *(209-532-0150)*. Beautifully preserved, this 12-square-block outdoor museum lets you really feel the atmosphere of the gold rush—minus the whiskey-soaked miners and ladies of the evening. Peek into a school, newspaper office, Cheap Cash Store, and church, and see the stagecoach office where a blackboard ticks off the schedule to Squabbletown and other gold camps. Visitors can ride a stagecoach *(fee)*, pan for gold *(fee)*, tour a mine *(fee)*, and see a museum focused on historical restoration.

Return to Calif. 4 and head for **Murphys** ★, which isn't much more than a few streets in the shade of cottonwood and locust trees. The guest register at the 1856 **Murphys Historic Hotel and Lodge** *(457 Main St. 209-728-3444)* was signed by Ulysses S. Grant and Mark Twain. Note the old bullet nicks around the door of the hotel saloon, which is still lively (but not *that* lively). Enjoy the clutter of relics at the **Old Timers Museum** *(470 Main St. 209-728-1160. Fri.-Sun.)*, which occupies an 1856 building and survived three fires, thanks to stone walls, iron shutters, and 6 inches of sand on the roof.

At ❺ **Calaveras Big Trees State Park** ★ *(209-795-2334. Adm. fee)*, farther along the route, trails wind among giant sequoias that have been tourist attractions since the 1850s.

101

Ahead, amid the granite peaks and evergreens of the High Sierra, lies **Bear Valley,** a hub of winter skiing and summer hiking and biking. *(Note: In winter Calif. 4 is closed beyond the ski resort.)* Continue to **Lake Alpine** *(209-795-1381)* for fishing and camping among firs and pines; you might see deer or even a black bear.

The road winds over Ebbetts Pass (8,731 feet), where the terrain recalls the Alps. At Calif. 89, go north. In the old lumber town of **Markleeville** there's a small museum with a log jail. Nearby **Grover Hot Springs State Park** *(4 miles W of town, Hot Springs Rd. 530-694-2248. Fee)* has a concrete pool filled with naturally heated mineral water for soaking.

Sunrise over Emerald Bay, Lake Tahoe

102

Continue on Calif. 89, past the T-junction where it bears northwest. Ahead you come upon what Mark Twain called the "fairest picture the whole earth affords" — ❻ **Lake Tahoe** ★ ★ *(Chamber of Commerce 530-541-5255, U.S. Forest Service 530-573-2600).* Its sparkling waters, cradled between the Sierra Nevada and the Carson Range, reach a depth of 1,645 feet; if drained, the lake would cover all of California with 14 inches of water.

As you drive along the western lakeshore, stop to see the turn-of-the-century summer estates of San Francisco's smart set at **Tallac Historic Site** ★ *(530-541-5227. Grounds year-round, museum Mem. Day–Sept.; building tours Mem. Day–Sept.; fee for tours).* Continue north to glacier-carved **Emerald Bay** ★ ★. The wooded bay resembles a fjord, and what looks like a Scandinavian castle on shore is **Vikingsholm** ★ *(530-525-7277. Mid-May–Oct.; adm. fee. Guided tours),* accessible via a steep, 1-mile path. Built in 1929, the 38-room mansion sports dragons' heads and a sod roof that blooms with wildflowers.

Winding farther north along the lake, you'll pass by popular **D.L. Bliss State Park** ★ *(530-525-7277. Adm. fee),* with hiking trails and odd rock formations. Ahead, watch Steller's jays flit through sugar pines and incense cedars at

Sugar Pine Point State Park ★ *(530-525-7232. Adm. fee).* To see where a wealthy banker passed his summers early this century, visit the **Ehrman Mansion** *(July–Labor Day; adm. fee),* built of stone and wood with a broad porch.

Drive on 9 miles to **Tahoe City,** stopping at the **Gatekeeper's Museum** and **Marion Steinbach Indian Basket Museum** *(130 W. Lake Blvd. 530-583-1762. May-Sept., tours by appointment April and Oct.; donation),* where you'll see pioneer relics and 800 Indian baskets. Nearby is the mammoth lake's only outlet, through a 1910 dam; the best view is from **Fanny Bridge,** named for the rear guard of sightseers lined up along its length. The town's oldest building is the furnished 1909 **Watson Cabin Living Museum** *(560 N. Lake Blvd. 530-583-8717. Mid-June–Labor Day);* its resident family was often visited by Washoe Indians who used the grinding stone out front.

Leaving Lake Tahoe behind, take Calif. 89 past the ski resorts of **Alpine Meadows** and **Squaw Valley.** The route runs beside the trout-filled **Truckee River** to I-80. Detour a couple of miles west to **Donner Memorial State Park** ★ *(530-582-7892. Adm. fee),* located where the ill-fated Donner party became snowbound during an early winter in 1846. Of 89 people trapped in the freeze, nearly half died—the survivors were driven to cannibalism. The **Emigrant Trail Museum** *(Adm. fee)* looks at the western migration of the 1840s, the Donner party, and the Central Pacific Railroad. In the park you can hike, camp, and enjoy Donner Lake.

East on I-80 lies **7** **Truckee** *(Chamber of Commerce 530-587-2757).* Built by the transcontinental railroad, the easygoing town has historic buildings along Commercial Row. East of town, pick up twisty Calif. 89 and head north; at tiny Sierraville the route melds with Calif. 49. You enter the wide **Sierra Valley,** explored in 1851 by black mountain man James Beckwourth. In this elongated depression between geologic faults, you'll see ranches and big empty spaces.

Past Graeagle the drive winds to **8** **Plumas-Eureka State Park** ★ *(530-836-2380),* via Calif. 89 and Route A-14. In the rugged, scenic area around 7,447-foot **Eureka Peak,** you'll find lovely hiking and a campground with a stream running through it. This is old mining territory, so explore the stamp mill, an 1890s house,

Tahoe sunbathers

Mother Lode and the Sierra

and the site of some of the Western Hemisphere's first competitive ski events; some historians claim the aerial tram system that carried ore was used as the world's first ski lift. A museum *(daily Mem. Day–Labor Day, weekends winter; adm. fee)* has mining equipment and preserved local animals, including a golden eagle and black bear. Also here is **Johnsville,** an old mining town with wooden buildings.

For the return, you can take Gold Lake Forest Highway *(closed in winter)* south from Graeagle; it becomes Gold Lake Road, ending up at Calif. 49.

A mile before Sierra City, stop at the **Sierra County Historical Park and Museum at the Kentucky Mine** *(530-862-1310. Mem. Day–Labor Day Wed.-Sun., Oct. weekends; adm. fee).* This 1850s hard-rock gold mine operated for a century; its working stamp mill is powered by water and Pelton wheels. Museum exhibits look at mining, skiing, logging, and Chinese settlers.

Sierra Buttes, near Sierra City

The road winds to picturesque ● **Downieville** *(Chamber of Commerce 530-993-6900 or 800-200-4949),* which straddles the Yuba and Downie Rivers. Brick and stone buildings on Main Street date from the gold rush. If you haven't had your fill of mining relics, visit the **Downieville Museum** *(330 Main St. Mem. Day–Labor Day),* which occupies an 1852 Chinese store and gambling house. Behind the courthouse stands an original **gallows,** used just once—to hang a murderer in 1885. The **Downieville Foundry** *(530-289-1020. By appt. only)* made equipment for local mills.

In North San Juan, make a 16-mile side trip to **Malakoff Diggins State Historic Park** ★ *(Via Oaktree Rd., left on Tyler Foote Crossing Rd. to Cruzon Grade, then follow signs. 530-265-2740. Adm. fee).* Rarely will you see land more ravaged than the Malakoff Pit, a gash in the earth 7,000 feet long by 3,000 feet wide, created by powerful water nozzles. Here, at what was once the world's largest

104

hydraulic mine, monitors blasted away whole mountain-sides to uncover deep gold deposits. The banded reddish terrain is weirdly beautiful. In the old mining town of **North Bloomfield** are partially restored buildings from boom days. You can hike and camp, plus swim in a lake.

Continue south on Calif. 49 to ⑩ **Nevada City** ★ *(Chamber of Commerce 530-265-2692)*, set in pine-clad hills. Downtown shows off gold rush buildings, illuminated at night by natural gas streetlights. On Broad Street stand the three-story **National Hotel** (1856) and the brick **Nevada Theatre** (1865), where Mark Twain gave a talk. Below the Victorian bell tower of the gingerbreaded Firehouse No. 1 is the **Nevada County Historical Society Museum** *(214 Main St. 530-265-5468. Nov.-April closed Wed.)*, which shows Indian artifacts, an 1880s Chinese joss house, and spoons from the 1846 Donner party.

It's a quick jump on busy Calif. 49/20 to **Grass Valley** *(Chamber of Commerce 530-273-4667)*, with its old commercial buildings on Mill and Main Streets. At the **North Star Mining Museum** *(Allison Ranch and McCourtney Rds. 530-273-4255. May–mid-Oct.; donation)* the world's largest Pelton wheel was used to generate power for hard-rock mining operations—the method of extracting gold ore buried in quartz veins through physical and chemical means; you'll also see a "man skip" that carried workers down into the mines. It's difficult to believe what's beneath your feet at **Empire Mine State Historic Park** ★ *(10791 E. Empire St. 530-273-8522. Adm. fee)*—367 miles of tunnels and shafts, some nearly 5,000 feet deep, that extend half a mile below sea level. Gaze down the main shaft of California's oldest and richest hard-rock mine, which produced 5.8 million ounces of gold. Also see the mine owner's 1897 summer home, modeled after a Cornish hunting lodge.

Pioneer artifacts at Downieville Museum

Ahead on Calif. 49, bustling ⑪ **Auburn** preserves its old town with an 1893 firehouse and 1849 neoclassic courthouse. The **Gold Country Museum** *(Gold Country Fairgrounds, 1273 High St. 530-889-4134. Closed Mon.; adm. fee)* has a model mine tunnel and a working miniature stamp mill. At the **Bernhard House** *(291 Auburn-Folsom Rd. 530-889-6500. Closed Mon.; adm. fee)*, docents in costumes re-create Victorian days amid period furnishings.

From Auburn, return to Sacramento via I-80 W.

Lake Tahoe and the

● **300 miles** ● **3 to 4 days** ● **Fall through spring**

Map labels:
CALIF.
395
To Pyramid Lake, 16 miles
395
TOIYABE N.F.
445
CALIFORNIA TRAIL (TRUCKEE ROUTE)
80
★❶ Reno — Sparks
Truckee
TAHOE
Verdi
N E V A D A
89
80
TOIYABE N.F.
395
NATIONAL
431
395
341
❼★★ Virginia City
50
Mt. Rose 10,776 ft
Washoe L.
342 Gold Hill
Silver City
Truckee
FOREST
Incline Village ❷
341
50 Dayton
89
PONDEROSA RANCH
28 LAKE TAHOE NEVADA S.P.
50 Carson City ★
CALIFORNIA TRAIL (CARSON ROUTE)
❸
89
Lake Tahoe ★★
28
Spooner Lake
50 ❻ ★
50
395
❹ ❺ Genoa
Zephyr Cove
206
Stateline
Minden
See p. 92
207
206 88
0   10 mi
0   15 km
N
50
ELDORADO N.F.   TOIYABE N.F.
395

Setting out from Reno's friendly urban canyons, lined with slot machines and wedding chapels, this drive climbs to Lake Tahoe, the largest alpine lake in North America. After tracing the piney shoreline past beaches and parks, the route descends from the south end of the "Lake in the Sky" to the Carson Valley and Nevada's oldest town, Genoa. Next comes the state capital, Carson City. Then it's off to meet the queen of the Comstock Lode, Virginia City, a dance hall girl whose face has been nicely lifted through historic preservation. From here, the route returns to Reno with a possible side trip to Pyramid Lake, the haunting remnant of an ancient inland sea.

For gambling and glitter, ❶ **Reno ★** *(Visitor Center 702-775-7366 or 800-367-7366)* is definitely the "branch office" compared to Las Vegas—and that suits many visitors just fine. Started as a railroad town in 1868, it became a supply center for silver miners of the Comstock Lode and still has a pleasantly small-time Western feeling. Early this century, Reno grew notorious for quickie divorces, bringing the rich and famous to await their decrees. Gambling boomed after Nevada legalized it in 1931—a mere formality since everyone was doing it anyway.

Near the Truckee River lies the downtown area, where the city's emblematic welcoming arch—emblazoned "Reno: The Biggest Little City in the World"—lights up the night. It marks the **Strip ★** *(N. Virginia St. between 1st and 6th Sts.),* the city's hub of gaming (Nevada public relations folk no longer say "gambling," which sounds chancier and less wholesome).

If your idea of one-armed sports doesn't involve pulling the handle of a slot machine, take in a tournament at Reno's state-of-the-art **National Bowling Stadium** *(300 N.*

Comstock★★

Center St. 775-334-2600). Located just east of the Strip, this Taj Mahal of Tenpins has 80 championship lanes and giant video replays. Nearby, the nervous gambling novice can plunk down five bucks for a ticket and a 90-minute lesson at the **Reno–Tahoe Gaming Academy** *(300 E. 1st St. 775-329-5665).* Keep moving south to a 220-plus car traffic jam of history at the **National Automobile Museum★** *(10 Lake St. S. 702-333-9300. Adm. fee),* where period streets and galleries showcase more than a century of automobiles, including such standouts as a 1907 Thomas Flyer and Buckminster Fuller's experimental Dymaxion, as well as the ba-a-a-d black 1949 Mercury coupe that James Dean drove in *Rebel Without A Cause.*

Nothing to do today? Bored? You can always get married at one of the city's wedding chapels after getting a license at the **Washoe County Courthouse** *(S. Virginia and Court Sts. 702-328-3275. Fee for license).* Nearly 30,000 marriage licenses are issued annually—about 80 percent to visitors.

For cultural treasures, Reno offers several nuggets north of downtown. The **Fleischmann Planetarium** *(Northern end of UNR campus, N. Virginia St. 775-784-4811. Adm. fee)* offers star shows, telescope viewing, and an exhibit hall where you can touch a meteorite—a true

Reno's skyline at dusk

UFO from space. Next door, the **Nevada Historical Society** *(1650 N. Virginia St. 775-688-1190. Closed Sun.; adm. fee)* traces the past through Washoe baskets by famous basketmaker Dat-so-la-lee, miners' gear, ranching equipment, and early slot machines. Other exhibits focus on famous Nevada residents Mark Twain and Bugsy Siegal. To the west at the **Wilbur D. May Museum★** *(1502 Washington*

St. 775-785-5961. Closed Mon.-Tues. fall and winter; adm. fee), you'll marvel at a shrunken head, Tang Dynasty horse sculptures, African masks, and more, collected by a May Department Stores heir and world traveler. The adjacent **Wilbur D. May Arboretum and Botanical Garden** *(775-785-4153)* shows what grows in the rugged transitional zone between the Sierra Nevada and the Great Basin. The Rose Garden features a unique collection of miniature, tea, heritage, and climbing roses, while the Burke Garden is styled after an English country garden. Don't miss the songbird garden.

Take US 395 south, then head west on Nev. 431. The road climbs past ski resorts and Mount Rose (10,776 feet), and after 21 miles reaches a scenic viewpoint overlooking **Lake Tahoe** ★ ★ *(Chamber of Commerce 530-541-5255)* and the snowcapped peaks that surround it. The lake, set in a deep bowl between the Carson Range and the Sierra Nevada, contains 39.8 trillion gallons of pure mountain water. It's so clear that you could see a dinner plate at a depth of more than 65 feet. Passing through ❷ **Incline Village,** an upscale ski and golf resort, take Nev. 28 south along the shore.

Reno glitz

If you were a fan of television's *Bonanza,* pull up your horse just ahead at **Ponderosa Ranch** *(775-831-0691. Late April–Oct.; adm. fee).* Little Joe and Ben Cartwright's hats hang on the rack in the ranch house where the show was filmed. Wander the Western town set, but be prepared for tourist trappings—staged gunfights *(Mem. Day–Labor Day),* Hossburgers, and an antigravity mine.

Four miles south of Incline Village, enter ❸ **Lake Tahoe Nevada State Park** *(775-831-0494).* The most popular attractions are the beach and shallow water at **Sand Harbor** ★ *(Adm. fee).* About 10 miles south is the turnoff for **Spooner Lake** *(775-831-0494. Adm. fee)* and its nature trail. From here you can enter a 14,000-acre backcountry that's popular for mountain biking, notably on the top-rated **Flume Trail** ★ overlooking Lake Tahoe.

Continue past ❹ **Zephyr Cove,** home port of the **M.S. Dixie II** *(Zephyr Cove Resort. 775-588-3508. Call for seasonal hours; fare),* the lake's newest and largest cruise boat.

Down the road lies the **Edgewood Tahoe Golf Course** *(Lake Pkwy. 775-588-3566. May-Sept., reservations required; greens fee)*, one of the nation's best public courses (according to *Golf Digest*), with nearly a mile of lake frontage.

Bottles, Nevada State Museum

Just before the casinos and showrooms of Stateline, turn east on Nev. 207 (which locals call Kingsbury Grade). Part of the 1860 Pony Express route, this scenic road climbs through evergreens over 7,334-foot Daggett Pass, then plummets nearly half that elevation in just 6 miles to the Carson Valley.

Turn north on Foothill Road (Nev. 206) and drive 4 miles to ❺ **Genoa★**. Founded on the California Trail in 1851 by Mormon traders, this is Nevada's oldest settlement and still a sleepy, tree-shaded bump in the road. Look at the 1886 **Genoa Town Hall** *(2287 Main St.)*; originally a dance hall, it's one of 30 Genoa buildings on the National Register of Historic Places. The 1851 trading post has been re-created as **Mormon Station State Park** *(Main St. at Genoa Lane. 775-782-2590. Mid-May–mid-Oct.)*, featuring a museum of Genoa life and an old wagon shelter with antique wagons. The Pony Express, railroads, and George Washington Gale Ferris, the local inventor of the Ferris wheel, are subjects at the **Genoa Courthouse Museum** *(Main and 5th Sts. 702-782-4325. Mid-May–mid-Oct.; donation)*. Pull up a stool at "Nevada's Oldest Continually Operating Thirst Parlor," the **Genoa Bar** *(2282 Main St. 775-782-3870)*, which dates from 1853.

Leave town on Genoa Lane, heading east to US 395, then north through cattle country to ❻ **Carson City★** *(Visitor Center, 1900 S. Carson St. 775-687-7410 or 800-638-2321)*. This supply hub for the mines of the Comstock Lode became the state capital in 1864. To see 19th-century buildings, get a Kit Carson Trail brochure from the Visitor Center.

Start your visit on the south edge of the city with a steam blast into the past at the **Nevada State Railroad Museum** *(2180 S. Carson St. 775-687-6953. Wed.-Sun.; adm. fee)*, home of locomotives and cars that in the late 19th century hauled Comstock ore on the Virginia & Truckee Railroad. Rail equipment is fired up for short excursions on weekends May through September *(fare)*. Inmates at the state prison graciously provided the quarried sandstone for the 1871 **Nevada State Capitol** *(Carson and Musser Sts. 775-687-4810)*, whose silver-colored cupola,

Mark Twain

In *Roughing It*, Mark Twain described his appearance while working for the *Territorial Enterprise* newspaper in Virginia City, one of the wildest settlements of the Wild West: "I was a rusty-looking city editor, I am free to confess—coatless, slouch hat, blue woolen shirt, pantaloons stuffed in boottops, whiskered half down to the waist, and the universal navy revolver slung to my belt. But I secured a more Christian costume and discarded the revolver. I had never had occasion to kill anybody, nor ever felt a desire to do so, but had worn the thing in deference to popular sentiment, and in order that I might not, by its absence, be offensively conspicuous, and a subject of remark."

visible as you drive north, represents the Silver State. Exhibits look at government history.

Carson City was the site of a U.S. Branch Mint (1870-1893), and even today something about a "CC" silver dollar says Old West. The mint, now the **Nevada State Museum**★ *(600 N. Carson St. 775-687-4810. Adm. fee)*, displays gold and silver coins, coin dies, money bags, a re-created mine, and a "ghost town" as it would have looked in the 1940s, before scavengers. Also, direct from the Ice Age, North America's biggest imperial mammoth.

Leave Carson City, drive east on US 50 to Nev. 341, and turn north. At the next fork take Nev. 342 into **Gold Canyon,** at whose mouth gold was discovered in 1849. It took a decade for prospectors to work their way uphill to the fabulous silver lode—dubbed the Comstock Lode—at Virginia City. During that time the canyon became a city of mines, mills, stores, homes, saloons, and fandango houses. You'll pass corrugated mine buildings, boarded-up shacks, old shafts, and mine tailings. It looks as if the hills had their innards turned inside out.

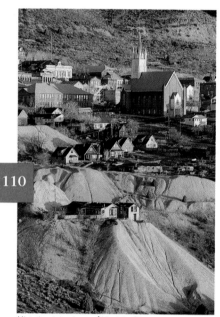

Historic mining town of Virginia City

110

Ahead lies historic ❼ **Virginia City**★★ *(Chamber of Commerce 775-847-0311. Some attractions close mid-Dec.–March)*. Born of the Comstock silver bonanza of 1859, its riches helped build San Francisco and finance the Union during the Civil War. Dinner houses served fresh oysters and French bubbly, while in 1880 more than a hundred saloons roared day and night. Start your visit on C Street, the boomtown's main drag. You can decide for yourself whether Virginia City has grown too commercialized.

Take a **mine tour** *(Chollar Mine, F St. 775-847-0155. Closed winter; adm. fee)* beneath the streets, where over 700 miles of tunnels perforate the hills. An impressively detailed model of the shafts and tunnels of the northern portion of the Comstock located directly beneath town are on view at **The Way It Was Museum** *(C and Sutton Sts. 775-847-0766. Adm. fee),* along with minerals, dolls in period dress, an old-time miner's shack, and a working scale model of a water-powered stamp mill like those that once crushed gold and silver ore.

When the **Fourth Ward School Museum** *(S. C St. and Nev. 342. 775-847-0975. May-Oct.; donation)* opened for students in 1876, its features included a central-heating system, running water on four floors, and attached bathrooms. Today, visitors sit at old desks and learn the history of Virginia City and the Comstock. There is also a small museum. If you're a fan of Samuel Clemens, make a pilgrimage to his desk at the **Mark Twain Museum** *(Territorial Enterprise Bldg., 47-53 S. C St. 775-847-0525. Adm. fee),* which houses an 1880s newsroom, including old printing presses, cases of type, and other memorabilia. Clemens first used the name Mark Twain as a *Territorial Enterprise* reporter in 1863 (see sidebar p. 109).

Also fascinating is the **Nevada Gambling Museum** *(22 S. C St. 775-847-9022. Adm. fee),* with its faro tables, hazard wheels, and crooked dice. When card sharps got caught, they sometimes played the "fifth ace," a concealed Derringer, such as those on display. Among more than a hundred antique slot machines, one truly symbolizes Western gambling—a one-armed bandit shaped like a masked badman; you pull his arm to spin the reels.

To get a feeling of the old days, wander the residential streets. One opulent home, built in 1868 by Robert Graves, superintendent of the Empire Mine, is the **Castle** *(70 S. B St. 775-847-0275. Mem. Day–Oct.; adm. fee),* decorated with rock crystal chandeliers; doorknobs made of silver; and Italian, French, and English furniture. John W. Mackay was the richest of the Comstock silver kings, and about 1860 he built the white-trimmed brick **Mackay Mansion** *(129 S. D St. 775-847-0173. Adm. fee).* Inside are original plush furnishings, Tiffany silverware, elegant bedrooms, and a Chinese laundry.

Steam trains of the **Virginia & Truckee Railroad** *(F St. Depot. 775-847-0380. May-Oct.; fare)* run to Gold Hill. In mining days, the railroad hauled lumber and supplies to miners and silver and gold ore to mills along the Carson River. End your visit at the northeastern edge of town with a stroll through the **Silver Terrace Cemeteries** *(775-847-0311),* whose headstones tell tales of hardship and danger: women who died in childbirth, men killed in mining accidents. All created the legacy of Virginia City. Return to Reno via Nev. 341 and US 395.

Pyramid Lake ★

From Reno, a side trip takes you across desert mountains to **Pyramid Lake** *(36 miles N via Nev. 445. 775-574-1000. Adm. fee; permit required for all uses).* In 1844 explorer John C. Frémont named the lake for a tufa island on the eastern shore that resembles the Great Pyramid of Cheops. The 28-mile-long lake is the vestige of an inland sea called Lake Lahontan; along its shore, prehistoric Indians wore robes of skins from American white pelicans—birds that still colonize Anaho Island (no approaches within 500 feet). The endangered, prehistoric cui-ui fish dwells in the lake, and nowhere else. **Sutcliffe** has a marina with a small museum; at nearby **Dunn Hatchery** *(Off Nev. 445. 775-476-0500. Call for schedule)* Paiute Indians raise Lahontan cutthroat trout for stocking.

111

● 530 miles ● 4 days ● Spring through fall ● Fill your tank when you can; gas stations are sparse.

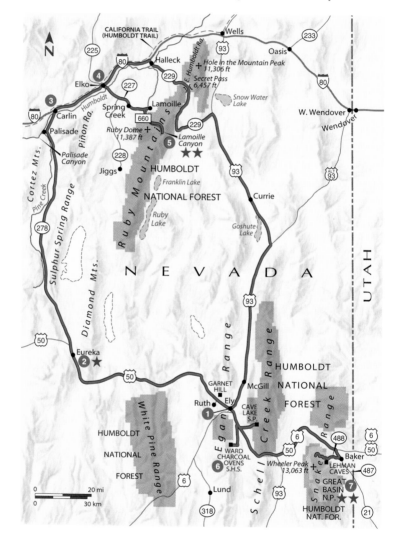

Out on Nevada's northeastern frontier, you might as well turn the car radio up, roll the windows down, and sing old rock 'n' roll at the top of your lungs. Nobody much will hear you anyhow. In this wide-open country, there might not be another car for miles and miles. Don't be abashed to sing out of tune, watch the skies for flying saucers, or speak frankly to the stars.

This looping ribbon of blacktop unspools across dry

basins and over ragged ranges—a surprisingly affecting
landscape tinted with the gray-green of sagebrush, the
golden straw of tumbleweeds. It's a different version of
Nevada, not what you see from the top floor of a Las
Vegas hotel. The route begins in the former copper and
railroad center of Ely. Heading west on US 50, "The
Loneliest Road in America," you drive to 19th-century
Eureka. Just beyond, turn north on a long, townless
stretch to Carlin, an old railroad town. Next travel east
along the Humboldt River to Elko, where the historic California Trail and the superhighway blend. From here a
side trip visits the gorgeous gorges of the Ruby Mountains. Then make a long run down nearly deserted US 93,
looping back to Ely and civilization. From here, visit
Great Basin National Park, whose bristlecone pines
are among the oldest living things on earth.

Mining recently started up again, but things got
awfully quiet in ❶ **Ely** *(Chamber of Commerce 775-
289-8877)* after the Kennecott Copper Corporation
closed its mine in 1983. The company left behind
its mine-to-smelter railroad, whose first locomotive
steamed into town in 1906 adorned with sagebrush
wreaths. This historic short line is preserved as the
Nevada Northern Railway Museum★ *(11th St. at
Ave. A, East Ely. 775-289-2085. Mem. Day–Labor Day;
adm. fee).* In the depot, wood-and-brass ticket
windows still gleam. Shop buildings house 60
pieces of rolling stock, from muscular locomotives to a roving bunkhouse for workers and a
rare 1907 rotary snowplow for icy tracks. On the
Ghost Train of Old Ely *(Call for schedule; fare)*
steam locomotives pull cars through town—
including the working red-light district, whose
residents may wave enthusiastically—and out to
the old Keystone mining area. (Be prepared for
flying cinders if you ride in an open car.) A diesel engine
also pulls carriages through the Steptoe Valley.

Peek into the **White Pine Public Museum** *(2000 Ault-
man St. 775-289-4710. Donation)* to see dolls, mining gear,
Native American artifacts, and a dinosaur footprint.

Heading west out of Ely, US 50 passes immense
mountains of sickly yellowish-white tailings left over from
the copper operations. About 5 miles west of town, turn
right on a dirt road (opposite Nev. 44 toward Ruth) to

113

Pony Express reenactment

Garnet Hill. Walk to the summit and an outcrop of rhyolite studded with blood-red gems. Says a local, "If you know where to look, you can kick the dirt and find 'em."

Farther ahead, the highway parallels the former Pony Express route. In this open range you'll see genuine cowboys with honest stains on their hatbands and sagebrush smell on their clothes.

Processing silver and lead ore in the 1870s, the 16 smelters of ❷ **Eureka**★ *(Chamber of Commerce, Eureka Sentinal Museum building. 775-237-5484)* spewed a thick, black smoke that earned the town the nickname Pittsburgh of the West. All that is gone now, and since the early 1980s there's been a gold boom. Stroll around the well-preserved 19th-century buildings *(guide booklet available at chamber),* including the 1879 brick **Eureka County Courthouse** *(Main and Monroe Sts.),* with its pressed-tin ceiling and potbellied stoves. There's a horseshoe balcony at the 1880 **Eureka Opera House** *(10201 S. Main St. 775-237-6006. Mon.-Fri.),* where the stage curtain still advertises local businesses of 1924. Now quiet, the printing presses of a newspaper founded in 1870 are displayed at the **Eureka Sentinel Museum** *(Monroe St. and Ruby Hill Ave. 775-237-5010. Daily May-Sept., Tues.-Sat. Oct.-April; donation).* On the west side of town, out Ruby Hill Avenue, see five historic cemeteries (including Masonic and Odd Fellows) at **Graveyard Flat,** which early residents called Death Valley. It's too bad visitors can't explore Eureka's underground tunnels, connecting what were once breweries to the town's numerous saloons.

Hotel Nevada at dusk, Ely

About 3 miles beyond Eureka, roll north on Nev. 278 through valleys flanked by the Sulphur Spring Range and Diamond Mountains to the east, and the Cortez Mountains to the west. After 82 miles you see Palisade Canyon, cut through reddish black rock by the Humboldt River. In the near-ghost town of **Palisade,** idle railroad men in the 1880s are said to have sometimes staged fake "Wild West" gun-fights as trains pulled in from the East, making passengers too nervous to dine at the depot, but amusing the locals.

Ahead, the old railroad town of ❸ **Carlin** is now enjoying a gold boom. Turning east on I-80, you'll trace the **Humboldt Trail,** traveled by early explorers starting with Peter Skene Ogden in the 1820s. This path paralleling the Humboldt River became part of the 1840s California Trail for wagon trains, then the transcontinental route of the Central Pacific Railroad in the late 1860s.

❹ **Elko** *(Chamber of Commerce 702-738-7135)* is the hub of a new mining boom based on bioleach technology. Single-celled organisms "eat" gold sulfides and turn them into oxides, from which ore can be recovered by traditional processes—thus speeding up nature's schedule by thousands of years. At heart, Elko is still a cow town, albeit with a sensitive side. During the annual **Cowboy Poetry Gathering** *(Western Folklife Center 702-738-7508. Late Jan.–early Feb.; fee for events)* 10,000 people come to hear real cowpunchers recite their poetry of the West. (During this event, hotel rooms are at a premium from Wendover to Winnemucca.)

Storm over sagebrush

During the 1940s, Hollywood tenderfoot Bing Crosby imported a touch of glamour when he bought ranches in the area. On one spread a river flooded, inspiring his song verse: "Oh, this was pretty badda, but we wouldn't leave Nevada, oh, no . . ." A denim tuxedo identical to the one Crosby owned is on view at the **Northeastern Nevada Museum** *(1515 Idaho St. 702-738-3418. Donation),* which also has an 1860s Pony Express cabin and exhibits on local Basque culture and mining. As annual rent on the historic Halleck Bar, the museum pays one bottle of Beefeater's gin, always served during a big shindig.

Elko is the gateway for a side trip into the rugged **Ruby Mountains** *(Humboldt National Forest 702-738-5171 or 800-715-9379)*—often called the Alps of Nevada. Take Nev. 227 south and go through Spring Creek to where the road jogs northeast to **Lamoille,** a ranching community where the photogenic white Presbyterian church poses against a mountain backdrop. In winter helicopters lift off from town, taking skiers (expensively) to the hundreds of square miles of virgin powder high in the Rubies *(Ruby Mountain Heli-Ski Guides, Reds Ranch. 702-753-6867. Fee).*

Before reaching town, Lamoille Canyon Scenic Byway

Ancient bristlecone pine,
Great Basin National Park

(Route 660) branches off Nev. 227, leading south to

5 Lamoille Canyon ★★ *(Humboldt National Forest 775-752-3357 or 800-764-3359. Road closed in winter).* One of Nevada's most beautiful spots, this great chute of metamorphic rock with granite intrusions was carved by moving glaciers. Known as the Yosemite of Nevada, the valley wraps around 11,387-foot Ruby Dome. Along the scenic byway are viewpoints and picnic areas; side canyons, cirques, and moraines; and fishing holes and beaver dams along Lamoille Creek. You can drive 13.5 miles to the 8,800-foot elevation, where trails link to alpine lakes.

Return to Elko and continue east on I-80. At Halleck take Nev. 229 southeast over 6,457-foot Secret Pass, where there's a pleasant feeling of frontier solitude. When you reach US 93, go south to Ely.

(Alternatively, take I-80 to Wells and turn south on US 93, passing the East Humboldt Range. To the west look for Hole in the Mountain Peak, perforated with a natural window near the 11,306-foot summit.)

From Ely, the drive continues south on US 93, which is also US 50 and US 6 for a little while. Just ahead on US 93,

Snow-covered Wheeler Peak, Great Basin National Park

watch for the gravel Cave Valley Road, which leads 7 miles to the **6 Ward Charcoal Ovens State Historical Site.** In the sagebrush stands a line of six ovens, built in 1876 of native stone to make charcoal for the smelter at Ward. Each 30-foot-tall, beehive-shaped oven held 35 cords of pinyon pine, a quantity that required stripping 5 or 6 acres of forest. Step inside one of the echoing ovens and give a shout.

About 2 miles farther along US 93, turn left on Success Summit Road and drive 7 miles to reach **Cave Lake State Park** *(702-728-4467. Adm. fee)*. In winter and early spring, says a local, "don't bring a boat; bring a saw—to cut through the ice and go trout fishing." In summer, bring hiking boots and explore trails through a juniper- and pinyon-dotted landscape.

The drive continues east on US 50. After climbing over the Schell Creek Range, you see the impressive Snake Range with Wheeler Peak jutting into the sky—marking your final destination ahead at **7 Great Basin National Park** ★ ★ *(Via Nev. 487 and 488. 702-234-7331)*. The Great Basin is a territory of valleys and ranges stretching from California's Sierra Nevada to Utah's Wasatch Mountains. It has been compared to a sagebrush sea, dotted with "mountain islands," where higher elevations bring cooler air, more water, and plants and wildlife that couldn't survive below. The park contains such an island, rising from the hot desert flats to the 13,063-foot summit of Wheeler Peak. On the way up you'll discover a succession of natural habitats, from cactus—and jackrabbits—up to pine forests—and mule deer—and finally to alpine tundra.

Near the Visitor Center, which contains natural history displays about the region, visit **Lehman Caves** *(Adm. fee. Bring a sweater)*. Dissolved out of native limestone by trickling water, the cavern extends a quarter mile and contains hanging curtains of stone and odd formations such as "cave popcorn" and helectites, which a Park Service brochure describes in a rare flight of wackiness as "forests of chow mein noodles." For perspective: It may take a century for a stalactite to grow a single inch.

Follow the 12-mile **Wheeler Peak Scenic Drive** *(Closed in winter)* to an elevation of 10,000 feet, where trails lead past alpine lakes and on a tough climb to the summit. One trail goes to a grove of bristlecone pines, among the oldest living things on earth; some have been on earth nearly 4,000 years. These gnarled trees are beautifully sculptured and polished by high wind carrying winter ice. They may remind you of other Western images—the classic sepia-tone photographs of American Indians, whose burnished faces reflect an immutable strength gained by outliving every trial.

Return to Ely the way you came.

Loneliest Road

It's 1860, and a lone Pony Express rider gallops through an empty territory of sagebrush valleys, blue skies, and weathered mountains. More than 130 years later, you parallel the same adventurous route along US 50. There still aren't many people or towns out here— the reason why *Life* magazine in 1986 dubbed the 287-mile stretch of US 50 between Ely and Fernley "The Loneliest Road in America." In response, communities along the route created a "Highway 50 Survival Kit," with a map that motorists can have stamped like a passport in the five biggest towns (Ely, Eureka, Austin, Fallon, Fernley). At the end, drivers are awarded a bumper sticker: 'I Survived Highway 50." Maps and kits are available from chambers of commerce in all five towns.

Las Vegas Recreational

● 170 miles ● 2 to 3 days ● Year-round; summer means Saharan heat in the desert parts of the drive.

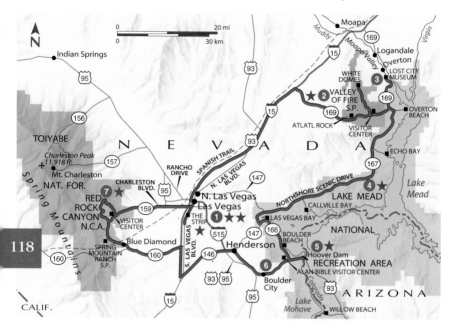

First take a dizzy spin down the Las Vegas Strip, where immense casino resorts are disguised as King Arthur castles and Egyptian pyramids. Here you play like a kid in the world's biggest sandbox, then (for virtuous enrichment) take in the city's museums. Next comes a loop through Nevada's southeastern corner. At Valley of Fire State Park, sunset touches the sandstone like a torch and a canyon hides Indian petroglyphs. You can go boating on Lake Mead and tour massive Hoover Dam. Next, explore Red Rock Canyon for the refreshment of wilderness. Then it's back indoors again, returning to the place that lounge comedians still call "Lost Wages."

You've arrived! Welcome to the city where hotels spring from the desert like neon exclamation points, where visitors stay up 24 hours a day rolling the bones and shouting incantations like tribal shamans, where magicians costumed in Liberace glitter suits make tigers vanish and slot machines make your dollars disappear, where buffet dinners offer 50 choices, where "enough" is never enough—

❶ **Las Vegas** ★ ★ *(Visitor Information Center 702-892-7575).*
As a nonstop party town, Las Vegas barely remembers

last night, much less history. But it has some: In January 1830, a Mexican trading party passed through Las Vegas Valley, then home to a series of natural springs and lush grasslands. *Las vegas* means "the meadows," and here explorer John C. Frémont camped 14 years later. His name is remembered not just in history books, but also in neon: Fremont Street, the heart of casino-lined Glitter Gulch downtown, has recently been transformed into a canopied, four-block-long, 2.1-million-bulb, high-tech light show called the Fremont Street Experience.

Historically, begin your visit at the north edge of downtown, where in 1855 Mormon settlers built an adobe outpost to shelter California-bound travelers. Today their vestigial **Old Las Vegas Mormon Fort State Historic Park** *(Las Vegas Blvd. N. and Washington Ave. 702-486-3511 or 702-486-5126. Call for hours; donation)* ranks as the oldest European settlement in Nevada. The Mormon parlor is furnished with 1850s items, and other exhibits include old photographs and drawings. Just south, the **Las Vegas Natural History Museum** *(900 Las Vegas Blvd. N. 702-384-3466. Adm. fee)* features an animated dinosaur exhibit, a 3,000-gallon tank full of sharks, and a room of live plants and wildlife native to Nevada's southwest desert.

119

Las Vegas Strip★ *(Las Vegas Blvd.)* begins around Sahara Avenue and stretches southward. A bit of history: Nevada legalized gambling in 1931, and ten years later the El Rancho Vegas Hotel-Casino opened on the two-lane highway from Los Angeles. After World War II, the

Casinos along the Strip

highway developed into the Strip, lined with "fabulous" casino-hotels. This building boom involved the Italian and Jewish crime syndicates and depended on newly available air-conditioning. Hotel showrooms presented celebrity entertainers like Frank Sinatra, as well as leggy showgirls with strategically placed feathers and rhinestones. This glitz had no competition until 1976, when

Atlantic City, New Jersey, legalized gambling. Las Vegas counterattacked by building full-blown destination resorts. Today the city boasts nine of the world's biggest hotels (the MGM Grand has 5,005 rooms). More behemoths are on the drawing boards.

On the Strip, nothing exceeds like excess. Near the corner of Tropicana Avenue and Las Vegas Boulevard, your mind struggles with a jumble of surreal architecture—a black pyramid entered through a massive sphinx (Luxor Hotel and Casino), a medieval castle with pennants flying (Excalibur Hotel Casino), the Manhattan skyline complete with a Coney Island roller coaster (New York-New York Hotel and Casino), and an entire 33-acre theme park (MGM Grand Hotel/Casino).

Bejeweled costume, Liberace Museum

Las Vegas offers some surprising bargains, including inexpensive hotel rooms and casino buffets. Of course, the casino-hotels have another way to get your money—gambling, which ranges from slot machines grinding away in noisy, smoky rooms, to private high-roller games where millions are won and lost in opulent surroundings. Underlying the action is one sobering fact: The county's casinos win nearly six billion dollars a year from some 4,000 gambling tables and more than 124,000 slot machines. This means somebody's losing.

Among the city's non-gambling attractions is the **Clark County Marriage License Bureau** *(200 S. 3rd St. 702-455-4415. Fee for ceremony).* A wedding takes place in Las Vegas every 5 minutes and 20 seconds—more than 100,000 a year. (It helps that a Nevada marriage involves almost no red tape, no blood test, and no waiting period.) After obtaining a marriage license, betrothed couples have a choice of 50 wedding chapels, many located in major hotels. Weddings range from black-tie affairs to an exchange of vows on a motorcycle. You can also join hands in the presence of a rhinestone-studded Elvis Presley impersonator.

South along the Strip is the **Imperial Palace Auto Collection** *(Imperial Palace Hotel, 3535 Las Vegas Blvd. S., 5th floor of parking facility. 702-731-3311. Adm. fee),* which displays more than 200 classic and historic vehicles, including the largest collection of Model J Dusenbergs in the world.

Two standouts: Benito Mussolini's 1934 Alpha Romeo and Elvis's 1976 Cadillac Eldorado.

A bit east of the Strip, visit the **Marjorie Barrick Museum of Natural History** (*Univ. of Nevada at Las Vegas, Harmon Ave. at Paradise Rd. 702-895-3381. Closed Sun.*), which has fossils, Native American artifacts, mounted birds, and live reptiles. Nearby, you'll discover that Mr. Showmanship isn't dead. The flamboyant, wildly popular pianist lives on at the **Liberace Museum** (*1775 E. Tropicana Ave. 702-798-5595. Adm. fee*). See his pianos (such as a Baldwin studded with 50,000 rhinestones), his glittering stage jewelry (including a ring designed like his trademark candelabra), and his costumes—feather-crested wonders resplendent with bugle beads and fur trim.

Also in the area is a truly odd combination—the **Ethel M. Chocolate Factory and Cactus Garden** (*2 Cactus Garden Dr. 702-433-2500*). Take a self-guided tour to see gooey goodies being made, then visit Nevada's biggest cactus garden, with 350 species of cactuses and succulents.

Now it's time to enter a different world, that of the Mojave Desert. Leave town on I-15/US 93; at Nev. 169 head east to ❷ **Valley of Fire State Park** ★ (*702-397-2088. Adm. fee*). In this 12-mile-long basin, ragged walls and spires of red sandstone rise against a turquoise sky—real Wild West scenery. Fanciful rock formations include the Beehives, Elephant Rock, and Grand Piano. After entering the park, stop at **Atlatl Rock** and climb an iron staircase to a sheer rock face carved with ancient petroglyphs. These pictorial records, including one of an atlatl (a spear-throwing stick), were left by the ancient Pueblo people, who lived here between 500 B.C. and A.D. 1150.

When you reach the Visitor Center, examine the geology and natural history exhibits. You'll learn that every square mile of this desertscape is home to thousands of living things, including gila monsters, roadrunners, Mojave desert sidewinders, desert bighorn sheep, and great horned owls.

Head north a mile from the Visitor Center to the **Petroglyph Canyon trailhead** and hike into the canyon, carefully checking its walls for prehistoric images. In this canyon you discover the park's beckoning silence, interrupted only by the grinding of your shoes on the sandy wash. (Warning: Temperatures can reach 120°F.)

A mile north from the trailhead lies **Rainbow Vista,** where red sandstone blends with white silica to yield pink,

Evolution of the Slot

The first slot machines appeared in 1890 in San Francisco. Instead of spinning reels, they used flipcards. Poker machines were the most popular. (Reels with varied symbols came later.) Manufacturers placed the machines in bars, describing them as "Trade Stimulators," and most paid off in cigars, drinks, or trade tokens. As late as 1901, a poker machine was granted a U.S. patent as an "educational appliance." Gradually the machines became unapologetic gambling devices. During the "golden age" of slots (1930-1950), their design incorporated polished aluminum cases and the full vocabulary of art deco—skyscraper forms, geometrics and chevrons, eagle wings. In 1964, the Bally "Money Honey" machine revolutionized the industry. It was lit up to lure customers in darkened casinos, and it announced winners with bells and jangling showers of coins—all designed, of course, to excite more play.

lavender, and purple rocks. About 3.5 miles farther at **White Domes,** you might spy chuckwallas or desert iguana basking in the sun near the cream-colored sandstone formations.

Continue through the park on Nev. 169 to the T-junction, and head north toward Overton. You're traveling through an area called the Pueblo Grande de Nevada, where the ancient Pueblo people lived in a 30-mile swath of sites before their mysterious disappearance around A.D. 1150. Learn about them at the ❸ **Lost City Museum** *(Just before Overton at 721 S. Nev. 169. 702-397-2193. Adm. fee),* where an extensive collection of artifacts—baskets, pottery, jewelry, tools—chronicles the history of settlement in this area from historic times to the present. A reconstructed pueblo is also open for tours.

Returning south on Nev. 169 to Nev. 167 (Northshore Scenic Dr.), head to the ❹ **Lake Mead National Recreation Area** ★ *(702-293-8990).* This blue wetness amid the beige grit seems a mirage, a vision hard to believe in a desert where people can die of thirst. Lake Mead is the largest man-made lake in the U.S., measuring 110 miles long and containing more than 9 trillion gallons of water. It stretches all the way to Arizona's Grand Canyon National Park. Camping, boating, fishing, and even scuba diving are major activities here. The lake's north shore is dotted with marinas—at Overton Beach, Echo Bay, and Callville Bay—where anything from a water-ski boat to a houseboat can be rented. On the water, drift lazily with rough cliffs towering above you, perhaps spotting a desert bighorn sheep.

Wild burro in Red Rock Canyon N.C.A.

Approaching Las Vegas Bay, go south on Nev. 166 (Lakeshore Scenic Dr.), passing **Lake Mead Cruises** *(Lake Mead Cruises and Ferry Terminal. 702-293-6180. Fare),* which offers cruises on the *Desert Princess* paddle wheeler; **Lake Mead Marina;** unshaded **Boulder Beach;** and the **Alan Bible Visitor Center** *(702-293-8990),* where you can pick up park information.

Take a left on US 93 to see the immovable object that created Lake Mead, ❺ **Hoover Dam** ★ *(702-293-8321 or 702-294-3521. Adm. fee).* Completed in 1935, this immense project—standing 726 feet high and 660 feet at the base—controls floods, generates electricity, and provides a reliable water source for about 25 million people. To construct the dam in this remote spot required the building of railroads, highways, and the "instant community" of Boulder City to house 5,000 workers. The amount of concrete alone used in its construction would build a sidewalk around the equator.

Tours begin at the Visitor Center, which has exhibits on electric power and Lake Mead. Tour groups ride an elevator down the equivalent of 53 stories to the dam's base, where they see the turbines and gaze up the sheer wall.

Now take US 93 west to ❻ **Boulder City** *(Chamber of Commerce 702-293-2034)*, the only town in Nevada where gambling is illegal. The **Boulder City/Hoover Dam Museum** *(444 Hotel Plaza. 702-294-1988. Adm. fee)* shows a film on the dam's construction and displays artifacts such as a bosun's chair used by workmen scaling the sheer wall.

Continue west; off US 95, take Boulder Highway north toward Henderson. Just before town, follow signs to the 26-acre **Clark County Heritage Museum** *(1830 S. Boulder Hwy. 702-455-7955. Adm. fee)*, where a timeline covers southern Nevada history from the Pleistocene epoch, when camels roamed the desert, to the modern phenomenon of Las Vegas. A street of historic structures includes the 1931 Boulder City Train Depot.

123

Lake Mead National Recreation Area

From Henderson, head west on Nev. 146, I-15, Nev. 160, and Nev. 159 to **Spring Mountain Ranch State Park** *(702-875-4141. Adm. fee)*. Here, natural springwater made the place a popular stop along the 19th-century Spanish Trail. In 1876, the land became a cattle ranch. It's cool here against the Spring Mountains, which is why Las Vegas locals picnic on the shady lawn beneath oaks and cottonwoods. The 1940s red ranch house, now a Visitor Center *(Fri.-Mon.)*, has old photos and furnishings.

Proceed north to ❼ **Red Rock Canyon National Conservation Area**★ *(702-363-1921)*, whose unspoiled sandstone canyons lie just 18 miles from the neon-and-glass canyons of Las Vegas. The Visitor Center has natural history displays. And here begins a 13-mile **loop scenic drive,** which wanders past a sandstone escarpment towering 3,000 feet high. Walking trails lead into narrow-walled gorges, where springs trickle (except in summer). Hikers can reach the **Keystone Thrust Fault,** which reveals a geological division between red sandstone and gray limestone. Return to Las Vegas via Nev. 159 (Charleston Blvd.).

● **120 miles** ● **1 day** ● **Year-round** ● **Speed limit never exceeds 55 miles per hour.**

Map labels:

Kahuku Point
Kawela
Kauai Channel
Sunset Beach
Waimea
PUU O MAHUKA HEIAU STATE MON.
Laie
Mokuauia I.
Pacific Ocean
WAIMEA BAY BEACH PARK
Kamananui Stream
KAHUKU
POLYNESIAN CULTURAL CENTER
Hauula
Waialua Bay
Haleiwa
WAIMEA FALLS PARK
KAWAILOA FOR. RES.
SACRED FALLS S.P.
Sacred Falls
Kahana Bay
Kaena Point
Opaeula Stream
Kahana
KAHANA VALLEY S.P.
Waialua
Kualoa Point
Wahiawa
Waikane
Waipio Acres
EWA
Kaneohe
Makaha
Kahaluu
Mokapu Point
Pokai Bay
BYODO-IN FOR. TEMPLE
Kaneohe Bay
Mokapu
Maili
Pearl City
Kaneohe
Kailua Bay
Kailua
O A H U
Nanakuli
Waipahu
Aiea
Koolau Range
RES.
Makakilo City
Pearl Harbor
BISHOP MUSEUM
NUUANU PALI OVERLOOK
Waimanalo Beach
U.S.S. ARIZONA MEM.
QUEEN EMMA SUMMER PALACE
KALAKAUA AVE.
PALI HWY.
MAKAPUU BEACH PARK
Makapuu Point
Ewa Beach
Honolulu
SANDY BEACH PARK
Barbers Point
Mamala Bay
Maunalua Bay
HALONA BLOWHOLE
FARRINGTON HWY.
Waikiki Beach
Diamond Head 762 ft
HANAUMA BAY STATE UNDERWATER PARK
Kaiwi Channel

Highway numbers: 83, 930, 93, 803, 801, 80, 99, 780, 750, H-2, 76, 95, 78, 63, 61, 92, 72, H-1, H-3

0   5 mi
0   10 km

N

This loop explores Oahu—"gathering place"—Hawaii's busiest and most populous island. Beginning in the tropical urban jungle of Honolulu, it then sets off on country highways that pass pineapple plantations, famous surfing beaches (with 35-foot-high waves), hidden waterfalls, and a sacred temple. The drive returns to the island's capital city after a pause at the much photographed Hanauma Bay.

Site of Kamehameha the Great's royal court in the early 1800s, ❶ **Honolulu** ★ *(Convention & Visitors Bureau, 2270 Kalakaua Ave. 808-923-1811)* grew into an important port for Pacific ships, developing as a tourist haven late in that century. In today's popular mind, Honolulu is pictured as a romantic travel poster—coconut palms waving above a crescent of sand where dark-eyed dancers sway under a big hula moon. In reality, its beachfront high-rises look more like Miami than a village of little grass shacks. A melting pot of Pacific and Asian cultures, the city has become a busy metropolis, one of the most fascinating in the nation, with historical and cultural riches to complement the "sun 'n' fun" of the beach.

Hawaiian royals once went to **Waikiki Beach**★ to surf and enjoy the breeze under the coconut trees. Today tourists descend to the beach from their towering hotels to broil in suntan oil, and ride gentle waves on outrigger canoes. Waikiki occupies less than a square mile but hums with the electricity of more than 95,000 people (both residents and tourists). The main drag, **Kalakaua Avenue,** is a whirling human kaleidoscope of honeymooners, sun-bronzed surfers, mayonnaise-white tourists from the mainland, Japanese tour groups, servicemen with buzz-jobs, moms and pops in matching aloha shirts, and party-hearty college kids. Souvenir shops sell enough T-shirts and puka-shell necklaces to accessorize every man, woman, and child in Missouri. The sensory overload is completed by Hawaiian steel-guitar music (piped in over loudspeakers) and the intoxicating fragrance of frangipani flowers.

If you want to have your picture taken while surfing

125

Waikiki Beach, Honolulu

on a wave of painted plaster, head for tourist-crammed **International Market Place** *(2330 Kalakaua Ave.),* whose stalls sprawl around a huge banyan tree.

A fun touristy touch is yours for free at the **Kodak Hula Show** *(Waikiki Shell, Kapiolani Park. Tues.-Thurs. 10* *a.m.),* which has been giving people a chance to use up film since 1937. Hula dancers demonstrate steps, then line up, holding the letters "A-L-O-H-A" for a classic photo souvenir. Kapiolani Park also holds the **Waikiki Aquarium** *(2777 Kalakaua Ave. 808-923-9741. Adm. fee),* whose residents range from sharks to chambered nautiluses and, of course, rainbow-colored tropical fish.

Diamond Head is the postcard-perfect backdrop to Waikiki, a ragged brow of tuff raised during an ancient volcanic eruption. It was named in 1825 by British sailors, who were later disappointed when the glittering crystals they'd found turned out to be only calcite. A trail leads up through dry scrub to the crater's rim (762 feet). On the way are a tunnel and gun emplacements from around World War I, when the U.S. Army envisioned Diamond Head as a mid-Pacific Gibraltar.

Waikiki Beach at sunset

Now explore Honolulu proper, west of Waikiki. Begin at the **Honolulu Academy of Arts** *(900 S. Beretania St. 808-532-8768. Closed Mon.; adm. fee),* which holds many surprises behind its thick lava-block walls: Flemish tapestries, van Gogh's "Wheat Field," the James Michener Collection of Japanese *ukiyo-e* woodblock prints, and Italian Renaissance paintings among them. Or catch a film or other performance at the Academy's theater *(808-532-8768. Adm. fee).*

Hawaii's earliest Christian evangelists built today's **Mission Houses Museum**★ *(553 S. King St. 808-531-0481. Tues.-Sat.; adm. fee)* in what is now downtown Honolulu. Featured are an 1821 house (the island's oldest standing frame house), a replica of a printing press that produced Hawaiian editions of the Bible and religious tracts, and a 1831 house built of coral.

Listen to the euphonious Hawaiian language during Sunday hymns across the street at the missionaries' **Kawaiahao Church** *(King and Punchbowl Sts. 808-522-1333).* Known as the Westminster Abbey of Hawaii, it was built in 1842 using 14,000 slabs of coral.

Lest you forget Hawaii was a monarchy, visit nearby **Iolani Palace**★ *(King and Richards Sts. 808-522-0832. Wed.-Sat.; adm. fee).* King Kalakaua's Italian Renaissance-style pile, completed in 1882, was inspired by European palaces (note the crimson-and-gold throne room), and

Sailing ship off Honolulu

featured the very latest gadgets (it had electricity before the White House in Washington, D.C.). The nation's only state residence of royalty, it served as capitol after 1893, when Kalakaua's sister and successor, Liliuokalani, was dethroned in a coup engineered by American businessmen and marines. Also on the grounds are the Coronation Pavilion and guard barracks.

In the waterfront area, the **Hawaii Maritime Center** ★ *(Honolulu Harbor, Pier 7. 808-536-6373. Adm. fee)* displays a replica of a Polynesian double-hulled voyaging canoe called *Hokule'a,* which has made long ocean trips. Ancient Polynesians navigated the vast Pacific without instruments or maps, guided only by stars and an astounding knowledge of ocean currents. Also displayed are model boats; whaling artifacts; a Matson liner stateroom; and the 1878 *Falls of Clyde,* the world's last full-rigged, four-masted sailing ship.

In nearby **Chinatown,** absorb the sights and scents of food markets and herb shops, buy leis (at prices much lower than in Waikiki), or dine. **Hotel Street,** a longtime haunt of off-duty sailors, still has girlie joints such as the Club Hubba Hubba, but the area is more interesting for reflecting Honolulu's international flavor, with Vietnamese, Thai, and Filipino eateries. Take one of the guided tours offered by the Chinatown Historical Society *(1250 Maunakea St. 808-521-3045. Mon.-Fri.; fee)* or the Chinese Chamber of Commerce *(808-533-3181. Tues.; fee).*

Close by, **Foster Botanical Garden** *(180 N. Vineyard Blvd. 808-522-7066. Adm. fee)* has more than 13 acres of

Kamehameha the Great

Born into a line of chiefs in 1758, Kamehameha I grew up to be good natured, humorous, and shrewd. It was his destiny to unify the Hawaiian Islands. After observing foreign ships and their superior weapons, Kamehameha obtained brass cannons. Invoking his war god in 1790, he began moving brutally through Hawaii, Maui, and Oahu. By 1810, Kamehameha controlled all the inhabited isles. Called the Lonely One, he ruled as a benevolent tyrant, maintaining peace and solidarity in the islands. When he died on Hawaii in 1819, he said: "Endless is the good that I leave for you to enjoy."

The Real Hula

To most of us, "hula" means a floor show with dancers shaking their grass skirts to the liquid music of steel guitars. But the real hula began as a religious ritual. Men and women used hand gestures, facial expressions, and dance steps to convey legends, love songs, and, of course, the natural world—the likeness of a swaying palm tree, hands fluttering down like rain. Although shocked Christian missionaries of the 1800s banished the dance, King Kalakaua—the "Merry Monarch"—saved it from extinction. After Hawaiian dancers were the hit of San Francisco's 1915 Panama-Pacific International Exposition, Tin Pan Alley began churning out popular tunes like "Yaaka Hula Hickey Dula," and Hawaii's image became a girl in a grass skirt. Watch out! In traditional hula, skirts are made of ti leaves or tapa—never grass.

trees that wall out noisy traffic. This green preserve, begun in 1853 when Queen Kalama leased the original property to physician and botanist William Hillebrand, contains tropical collections of fine palms and orchids. A stately Bo traces its roots to the tree under which the Buddha received enlightenment in India more than 2,000 years ago.

A short side trip north of the city takes you where Queen Emma and her family fled from the heat of Honolulu, the **Queen Emma Summer Palace** ★ *(2913 Pali Hwy. 808-595-6291. Adm. fee)*. An airy 1840s house of Greek revival style, it was shipped precut from Boston to this tropical setting. The house contains some original furnishings, including a set of china given to Emma by Queen Victoria and the carved cradle of Emma's and Kamehameha IV's beloved son, who died at age four.

From Honolulu, head west toward Pearl Harbor, but don't fail to stop at the amazing **Bishop Museum** ★ ★ *(1525 Bernice St. 808-847-3511. Adm. fee)*. Its 22 million specimens focus on natural history and island society, especially the cultural history of Polynesia and the Pacific. Exhibits include a model temple; royal feather capes; and Kamehameha the Great's own war god, an absolutely terrifying image bristling with dogs' teeth and flame-colored feathers. Also of interest are war clubs, musical instruments, Queen Liliuokalani's regal coach, samurai armor, Melanesian masks, a 55-foot model of a sperm whale, a planetarium, and much more.

Take H-1 west to **Pearl Harbor** and the ❷ **U.S.S. *Arizona* Memorial** ★ ★ *(U.S.S. Arizona Memorial exit. 808-422-2771. Arrive before noon to assure entry)*. At the Visitor Center, the date December 7, 1941, comes to life through exhibits featuring newspaper headlines; servicemen's training manuals and pinup photos; and a film about the Japanese attack on the U.S. Pacific Fleet, when 2,388 persons were killed, 8 ships sunk, and nearly 350 airplanes damaged. The submerged U.S.S. *Arizona*, an instant tomb for 1,177 crewmen, is today spanned by a white memorial. From its bridge, visitors gaze silently at the twisted metal beneath the water or set leis drifting or drop strings of tiny pearls that rest on the ravaged hull like pure white wishes for peace.

Nearby, the **U.S.S. *Bowfin* Submarine Museum and Park** *(808-423-1341. Adm. fee)* lets visitors clamber down the companionway of the "Pearl Harbor Avenger," a sub

Orchid, Foster Botanical Garden

that sank 44 enemy ships.

Follow Hawaii 99 north through Hawaiian suburbia, taking the bypass on Hawaii 80 through Wahiawa and continuing on Hawaii 99. Here pineapple fields stretch away in vast sections of yellowish green. Soon you will see the **North Shore,** one of the world's greatest surfing areas. Here, winter swells rush unimpeded across the Pacific, sometimes rising as high as 35 feet when they hit the coast.

Take Hawaii 83, pausing to buy coconuts or exuberant tropical flowers at roadside stands. At ❸ **Waimea Bay Beach Park**★ huge winter surf splashes your windshield with salt spray, while daredevil surfers ride the moving mountains of water. Just ahead is the turnoff to **Waimea Falls Park** ★ *(808-638-8511. Adm. fee).* Located up a green river valley, the park nourishes Hawaiian plants and traditions alike. There are gardens filled with more than 6,000 varieties of trees and flowers, including ginger and hibiscus. Also of interest are the reproductions of early Hawaiian thatched houses, and a diver who leaps from a 60-foot cliff into a pool below Waimea Falls. Hula demonstrations are authentic; no grass skirts here.

Returning to Hawaii 83, drive about a half mile to Pupukea Road and turn right, going half a mile to **Puu O Mahuka Heiau State Monument**★. Oahu's most extensive open-air temple *(heiau)* is terraced within low walls of volcanic rock. Among the human sacrifices reportedly made here were British crewmen under navigator George Vancouver in 1792. Today you'll see local people's offerings—usually *ti* leaves—made to the gods of old Hawaii. Not coincidentally, the site has a commanding view over the coast.

Continue on Hawaii 83 to **Sunset Beach**★, a famous surfing area. One break is the legendary Bonzai Pipeline. The road rounds Kahuku Point to Oahu's windward side,

Dancer at the Polynesian Cultural Center

where ahead lies the tour-bus-packed **Polynesian Cultural Center** *(808-293-3333. Closed Sun.; adm. fee)*. Seven authentically re-created villages represent cultures from Hawaii to Samoa to New Zealand. There are also demonstrations of crafts and poi pounding and an elaborate dinner show.

Continue in the shadow of the jagged Koolau Range. At **Sacred Falls State Park,** a trail leads 2 miles to an 80-foot

waterfall set amid towering cliffs. (Note: Flash floods and falling rocks have been hazards here.)

Farther ahead, turn off from Hawaii 83 to the ❹ **Byodo-In temple** *(Adm. fee),* a copy of a 900-year-old shrine in Japan, with a large Buddha inside. Set against the green Koolau Range, the temple is painted cinnabar with yellow trim. It's a perch for colorful peacocks, and the koi lake is peaceful—until you toss in some food, causing the orange and silver fish to flap in the water so vigorously it sounds like applause.

Byodo-In temple

When you reach Hawaii 61, turn inland to the **Nuuanu Pali Overlook ★,** with its legendary view straight down chiseled cliffs. Conquering warrior Kamehameha the Great supposedly drove Oahu's last defenders over these green palisades in 1795. If you're already having a bad hair day, lean over into the updraft. Some days the wind is so strong that rain-fed waterfalls actually blow uphill. In the distance lies windward Oahu, its populated areas set among swatches of tropical green and blue.

Return to the junction with Hawaii 83 and continue on Hawaii 61 to Hawaii 72; turn right. Ahead, **Makapuu Beach Park** is a bodysurfing spot where bone-jarring waves can be 12 feet high (experts only). Across the road, **Sea Life Park** *(808-259-7933. Adm. fee)* has performing dolphins and sea lions as well as a giant reef tank with almost 4,000 tropical fish. Its free whaling museum displays blubber-boiling kettles and items lonely whalers made of panbone (the lower jawbone of a whale) and whales' teeth, from canes to jagging wheels for wives back home to edge pie crusts. On display are beaks of giant squids, among 400 found undigested in the stomach of a stranded sperm whale. Whales can often be sighted from here as they pass offshore between November and April.

The white lighthouse ahead marks Oahu's eastern extremity, Makapuu Point. Around the bend, **Sandy Beach Park** has a strong shore break popular with experienced bodysurfers. Its sandy, unshaded strand is great for sunbathing. Drive on about 2 miles to the **Halona Blowhole,** named for a jet of water that shoots out of a rocky crevice, particularly when the sea surges. (It is connected to an undersea tunnel.)

No snorkeling spot in Hawaii is more popular than ❺ **Hanauma Bay State Underwater Park ★.** The reason? Sticking your head underwater here is like looking into an aquarium. Angelfish, parrot fish, and other colorful sea critters meander through the coral. The

Seacoast vista from Hawaii 72, near Honolulu

turquoise bay may look familiar—as it was at this very spot that Elvis Presley filmed the wonderfully cornball *Blue Hawaii.*

Take Hawaii 72 until it melds with H-1, which will bring you back to Honolulu.

Kauai ★★

● 150 miles ● 2 to 3 days ● Year-round ● Seek local advice before swimming; many beaches have treacherous riptides or other dangerous conditions.

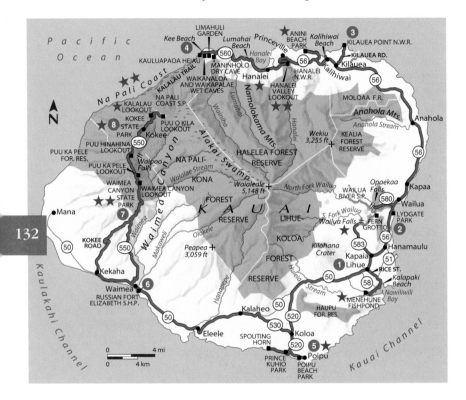

132

When Hollywood moviemakers want to film "paradise," they often come to Kauai, as they did for *South Pacific, King Kong,* and *Jurassic Park.* The island may be small (just 32 miles across), but it takes in mountain ranges, green valleys, sunny beaches, the majestic "Grand Canyon of the Pacific," Hawaii's only navigable river, and the famous Na Pali Coast—a stretch of coves and cliffs so rugged they can be reached only by hiking trail or boat. This coast blocks the island's perimeter road from completing a circle—a blessing, because this leaves whole regions of Kauai remote and unspoiled. All around the Garden Isle you'll find the towns small, the buildings no higher than a coconut tree (except for one hotel), and the people relaxed and friendly. Exploring all these wonders, this drive makes two different round-trips, north and south from centrally located Lihue.

An old sugar plantation town, **❶ Lihue** *(Convention & Visitors Bureau 808-245-3971. General information on Kauai also available)* is the island's commercial and civic center. The **Lihue Sugar Mill,** founded in 1849, still crushes sugarcane, harking back to the days when sugar was the island's main industry; a conveyor belt moving the sweet product straddles Hawaii 50 near Hawaii 56.

Want to see history close-up at an 1864 sugar plantation? Visit the **Grove Farm Homestead Museum★** *(Nawiliwili Rd. 808-245-3202. Mon., Wed., and Thurs., reserved tours only; adm. fee),* where you see humble workers' houses and the owner's mansion, with its walls of rich koa wood and displays of Hawaiiana and embroidery.

Downtown, a cluster of 1930s buildings dot Rice Street, the town's main thoroughfare. In one of them, the old library, you'll find the **Kauai Museum** *(4428 Rice St. 808-245-6931. Closed Sun.; adm. fee).* Here, the history of Kauai—the oldest Hawaiian island—is told, from its volcanic origins some six million years ago to 19th-century plantation life. Among the exhibits, a model village, quilts, feather leis, and hula instruments illuminate early Hawaiian culture; while seashells and gourds introduce the region's natural history.

In the town's watery frontyard on Nawiliwili Bay, **Kalapaki Beach** offers a lovely crescent of sand and good water for swimming and body-surfing. Kayakers start in the bay and venture up **Huleia Stream,** where jungle greenery grows to the water's edge. This lush landscape appeared in the Indiana Jones movie *Raiders of the Lost Ark.* Not far upstream via Hulemalu Road, the **Menehune Fishpond★** is set apart from Huleia Stream by stone walls that may have been built more than a thousand years ago by Hawaii's first settlers, the *menehune.* Legend says these "little people" did the work in a single night, passing stones one to the next for 25 miles. An adjacent marshy area is a refuge for native birds such as Koloa ducks and Hawaiian black-necked stilts.

Opaekaa Falls, near Wailua

Four miles north of Lihue via Hawaii 56 and 583, you'll find **Wailua Falls★,** where two 80-foot cascades drop side by side over a sheer cliff. If you're willing to admit you watched TV's *Fantasy Island,* you'll recognize these falls from the opening credits. According to legend, island chiefs made ceremonial leaps to prove their courage.

Return to Hawaii 56 and drive north about 5 miles to the mouth of the **Wailua River,** the only navigable waterway in the Hawaiian Islands. On the south side of the river mouth, ➋ **Lydgate Park** offers fine snorkeling among resident blue parrot fish, a grove of ironwood trees, and two large pools framed by lava rocks. There are traces of a *heiau* (temple) and the **Hauola Place of Refuge,** where a violator of old Hawaiian taboos—perhaps a commoner who allowed his shadow to fall on a chief—could escape execution.

Accompanied by enthusiastic musicians singing such local favorites as the "Hawaiian Wedding Song," you can take a boat tour upriver to a greenery-draped cave called the **Fern Grotto** *(808-821-6892 or 808-822-4908. Fare).* Or take a **side trip**★ along the Wailua River, on Hawaii 580. After half a mile you'll see **Holoholoku Heiau,** the sacrifice spot for unlucky taboo violators who didn't make it to the place of refuge. Nearby, noble women bore their children at the flat-backed royal birthing stones. Keep driving inland; just past **Poliahu Heiau,** which once

134

Hanalei Valley, near Hanalei

belonged to a chief, is an overlook on lacy **Opaekaa Falls.** Well to the west, at the center of the island, is the Wailua River's source, Waialeale (5,148 feet). One of the wettest spots on earth, it receives an average 451 inches of rain annually.

Back on the main route, continue north on Hawaii 56 past Kapaa and Anahola to the 1870s plantation town of **Kilauea.** Here, head out Kilauea Road to Kilauea Point and the ❸ **Kilauea Point National Wildlife Refuge** *(808-828-1413. Adm. fee),* the domain of red-footed boobies, wedge-tailed shearwaters, Laysan albatrosses, and great frigatebirds with 7-foot wingspans. Look off-shore for sea turtles, dolphins, and—between November and April—humpback whales. Also at the refuge stands a 1913 **lighthouse.**

Waioli Huiia Church, Hanalei

About a mile west of Kilauea, take the first Kalihiwai Road you come to (there's another one just after) to **Kalihiwai Beach,** a wide strand on a pretty bay. The second Kalihiwai Road (and a left on Anini Road) will bring you to **Anini Beach Park ★,** a popular spot for snorkeling and learning to windsurf. It has miles of sand and a fring-ing reef that creates a quiet lagoon safe for swimming. (This beach used to be named Wanini, but the "W" fell off the sign, and nobody ever bothered replacing it.)

Continue on the coastal highway past Princeville. Just beyond the point where Hawaii 56 becomes Hawaii 560, pause at **Hanalei Valley Lookout ★ ★,** which overlooks geometrical taro fields threaded by the calm Hanalei River. The valley grows about half of Hawaii's taro root, which is pounded to make poi, the gooey finger food that mainlan-ders often compare to wallpaper paste. Partially protected as the Hanalei National Wildlife Refuge, the valley harbors four endangered native waterbirds—Hawaiian black-necked stilt, Hawaiian coot, Hawaiian moorhen, and Koloa duck.

Continue into the valley to **Hanalei ★,** a tiny town that devotees say has an otherworldly quality, as if the water faucets ran with magic potion. The area is home to a tropical punch blend of local families, surfers, celebrities, and New Age types. Explore the mountain-girded **Hanalei Bay,** which enjoys a worldwide reputation as a summer yachting port. It's a classic crescent of sand with streams running into the ocean.

For a glimpse of Hanalei's roots, see the 130-year-old clock that's still ticking at **Waioli Mission House** *(808-245-3202. Tues., Thurs., and Sat.; donation).* A Southern-style frame residence erected by missionaries in 1837, it is surrounded by a riot of jungle greenery seen through wavy glass windows. In front is the green **Waioli Huiia Church,** where Sunday hymns are sung in Hawaiian.

Just past town is **Lumahai Beach** *(Viewpoint past Milepost 4),* the location of the scene in *South Pacific* (1957) wherein Mitzi Gaynor vowed to "wash that man right out of my hair." Don't swim here, due to treacherous conditions.

136

Na Pali Coast at sunset

Keep driving across one-lane bridges. Within a few miles you reach **Maninholo dry cave,** said to have been dug by the menehune. Then comes **Limahuli Garden** *(808-826-1053. Closed Mon. and Sat.; reservations required for guided tours; adm. fee),* with native plants and taro growing on thousand-year-old rock terraces—a vision of Hawaii in early times. On ahead, Limahuli Stream is handy for rinsing off salt water and sand. Farther along the road are the **Waikanaloa** and **Waikapalae wet caves,** with pools of water inside.

The road ends at ❹ **Kee Beach.** Popular for swimming (only in summer during calm conditions), it also has a reef for snorkeling. A path leads along the cove, above the rocks, to ancient **Kauluapaoa Heiau,** where the sacred hula was taught to youths.

From Kee Beach, the **Kalalau Trail** snakes its way up and down cliffs to the Kalalau Valley, 11 miles along the **Na Pali Coast** ★ ★ *(808-274-3444. Permit required for camping or hiking beyond 2 miles. Hiking difficult and swimming often dangerous. Also accessible by boat and helicopter tours).* On this remote coast you'll discover the way Hawaii used to be, with green valleys, dramatic palisades, secluded beaches, and streams with pools and waterfalls. Hawaiian families were living in the timeless valleys of Na Pali by A.D. 1000. After a few hours here, you'll forget what century it is.

Retrace your route to Lihue for the second half of the drive, now heading south and west of town. Begin by driving southwest on Hawaii 50. After 7 miles, go south on Hawaii 520 to **Koloa,** where the first sugar mill in Hawaii was erected in 1835. All that's left are remnants of the old chimney. In this tourist-oriented town you'll see false-fronted buildings, huge poinciana trees, and cascades of scarlet bougainvillea.

Continue south on Hawaii 520 toward Kauai's main resort hotel area, Poipu. After 2 miles, turn right onto Lawai Road, leading to **Prince Kuhio Park** and the the 1871 **Birthplace of Prince Kuhio,** who became one of Hawaii's first territorial delegates to Congress. Farther along is the **Spouting Horn,** a tube in a lava shelf through which waves surge, sending up a fountain of spray. It first makes a strange rasping sound, which legend says is the moaning of a giant female lizard trapped in the tube by a clever fisherman.

In ❺ **Poipu★,** you'll want to visit **Allerton Garden★** *(808-742-2623 or 808-332-7361. Tues.-Sat., reservations required; adm. fee.),* a former private estate where the landscape has been turned into art. You stroll through outdoor "rooms" created by exotic tropical hedges and tree canopies, decorated with pools, fountains, and sculptures. The tour also explores part of the Lawai Garden, whose collection ranges from common bamboo to the rare plant *Kanaloa kahoolawensis;* only four are left in the world—two in the wild and two in the garden's nursery. Ask about the huge ficus tree where the dinosaur eggs were found in *Jurassic Park.*

Flower-laden truck near Eleele

Near the resort area, **Poipu Beach Park** offers golden sand and nice snorkeling.

Retrace your way to Koloa and take Hawaii 530 northwest to Hawaii 50, and continue west. Less than a mile before Waimea lies ❻ **Russian Fort Elizabeth State Historical Park,** which contains the ruins of an 1816 fort built by the Russian-American Company to provision its trading ships. The star-shaped bulwark was made of lava rocks, soon after abandoned, and now is in rubble and overgrown.

Ahead in **Waimea,** Capt. James Cook made his first landfall on the Hawaiian Islands in January 1778. Just west of town, turn north on Hawaii 550 (Waimea Canyon Drive), which winds up into the cooler interior of the

island. You're heading for ❼ **Waimea Canyon State
Park** ★ ★ *(808-274-3444)*, which preserves what Mark
Twain dubbed the "Grand Canyon of the Pacific"—a 3,600-
foot-deep gorge that opened along a geological fault and
then was eroded by streams and rain. The red earth does

Rugged coastline near Poipu

resemble the Arizona canyon, but is veiled by mists, acces-
sorized with greenery, and often trimmed with waterfalls.

Walk the **Iliau Nature Loop,** located before Milepost 9,
for a look at the canyon and its plants—particularly native
iliau, a cousin of the rare silversword, with a stem that can
be 12 feet tall. After Mile 10, stop at spectacular **Waimea
Canyon Lookout,** a viewpoint that shows stream-carved
side canyons entering the main, 10-mile-long gorge.
Ahead at **Puu Ka Pele Lookout** you can see 800-foot-high
Waipoo Falls (dry during rain shortages). **Puu Hinahina
Lookout,** past Mile 13, has viewpoints of the island of
Niihau—which is privately owned and almost purely
Hawaiian—and down the length of Waimea Canyon.

Soon the road enters ❽ **Kokee State Park** ★, high in
the mountains. The park's many hiking trails wander past
ginger, ferns, koa trees, and many other plants; a boardwalk runs over the boggy terrain of the Alakai Swamp.
You can obtain hiking information and arrange guided
hikes at the **Kokee Natural History Museum** *(808-335-
9975)*, located just past Mile 15. The museum also has a
3-D model of the canyon, plus displays on local plants,
animals, and hurricanes. Note the shell of a Pacific green
sea turtle, an animal revered by some Hawaiian families
as their *aumakua,* or ancestral guardian spirit. The facility
has been called a "bantam museum," not only for its size

but also for the wild chickens running loose outside. (They're actually *moa,* or jungle fowl.)

Don't miss driving on through the ohia forest to **Kalalau Lookout★**. Here, at 4,000 feet above sea level, you're at the altitude where clouds form; a clear view is more likely before 10 a.m. You look down the largest valley on the Na Pali Coast, a jumble of green land tumbling to the blue Pacific. Settled by ancient Hawaiians and populated until the 1920s, the valley's only residents now are wild pigs and goats, rummaging among the silvery green *kukui* trees. Another viewpoint overlooking the lush valley, the **Puu O Kila Lookout,** comes at road's end.

You have two choices for the trip back to Hawaii 50. Remain on Hawaii 550 alongside Waimea Canyon, the

Waimea Canyon

way you came; or turn right partway down on Kokee Road, which descends with varying views of the coast and the island of Niihau to the town of Kekaha. Hawaii 50 will then bring you back to Lihue.

Maui ★

● **200 miles** ● **2 days** ● **Year-round**

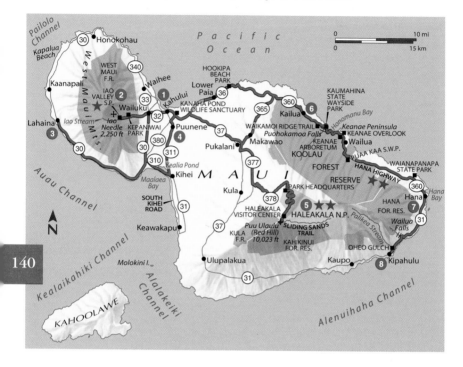

Sugarcane, pineapple, cattle—and tourists—are the
staple crops on Maui. It's the island of water fun, and its
visitors tend to gather at beach resorts along the southern
and western coasts. In winter, humpback whales gather
along these shores, too. The drive begins exploring the
island in the business hub of Kahului, then meanders into
the hushed green Iao Valley, whose name means "cloud
supreme." Next you visit the historic whaling town of
Lahaina before going on to the developed beach area
around Kihei. Crossing to the more rural east side of the
island, you ascend through the clouds to Haleakala
National Park, which surrounds a volcano 10,023 feet
high. Here the demigod Maui snared the sun so it would
linger over Hawaii. (The trick seems to have worked.) To
wrap things up, the drive follows the famous Hana Highway along the lush windward coast, where every curve
brings another gushing waterfall or tropical garden spot.

❶ **Kahului** (*Convention & Visitors Bureau 808-244-3530
or 800-525-6284. General info on Maui available*) serves as
the island's major transportation hub. From the port here

Maui's raw sugar and pineapples are shipped out. About a mile and a half west of the island's major airport is the **Kanaha Pond Wildlife Sanctuary** *(Off Hawaii 36 and the airport access road. 808-984-8100. Entry permit required),* whose marshy ponds play host to Hawaiian black-necked stilts, Hawaiian coots, herons, and ducks.

Follow Kaahumanu Avenue (Hawaii 32) west into adjoining **Wailuku** *(Convention & Visitors Bureau 808-244-3530 or 800-525-6284),* a small town set against the West Maui Mountains. The 1876 **Kaahumanu Church** *(W. Main and High Sts.),* with its white stone exterior, green roof, and clock-tower steeple, reflects the New England heritage of the early missionaries to the island; Sunday hymns are sung in Hawaiian. An 1833 girls' boarding school, later the residence of headmaster and painter Edward Bailey, is now the **Bailey House Museum** *(2375A Main St. 808-244-3326. Closed Sun.; adm. fee).* On display are his landscapes of the island; furniture of native koa wood; and Hawaiian artifacts from before European contact, including rare bark cloth and a spear edged with sharks' teeth for disemboweling enemies.

Nearby lies a lovely valley best known for an unlovely slaughter. In 1790, in what is now **Kepaniwai Park** *(Via W. Main St. and Iao Valley Rd.),* legend says that the invading forces of Kamehameha the Great wiped out warriors trying to defend Maui, and corpses actually choked the stream running through the Iao Valley. Today, park buildings focus on Hawaii's diverse cultures with reconstructions of a Japanese house, a Chinese pavilion sporting green dragons, a Portuguese house with a red-tile roof, and a Filipino house of bamboo. The new **Iao Valley Discovery Center** *(808-244-6500. Adm. fee)* has imaginative, hands-on exhibits that explain how plants and animals arrived in this archipelago and adapted to its environments.

1876 Kaahumanu Church, Wailuku

Just ahead is the ❷ **Iao Valley State Park★**, a lush gorge with trails and a stream. Often shrouded in mist, the **Iao Needle,** a weathered stone pinnacle, spears the sky, as it rises to a height of 2,250 feet.

From Wailuku, pick up Hawaii 30 and drive south through pineapple and sugarcane fields, then north along the coast to ❸ **Lahaina,** once the wild and wanton whaling capital of the Pacific. When Christian missionaries came in the 1820s and tried to tame the fun, sailors loosed a few

Iao Valley State Park

cannonballs at one of their homesteads. Today Lahaina has two distinct personalities—one of well-preserved historic buildings and another of well-stocked shops touting T-shirts, ice cream, and sentimental paintings of whales. Between November and April, you can see the leviathans in the flesh, as countless **humpback whales** ★★ come to these warm waters to breed and calve. Watch for the magnificent mammals offshore as they blow, breach, and lobtail.

The **Lahaina Historic District** ★ is clustered around the town's small harbor. Pick up a walking tour guide and information on sites at the Lahaina Restoration Foundation, located inside the **Master's Reading Room** *(Front and Dickenson Sts. 808-661-3262. Mon.-Fri.).* Sailors once came here to read in cool, quiet comfort. Other historic sites in the Front Street area include the furnished 1834 **Baldwin Home** *(Adm. fee);* a 1912 Chinese fraternal hall, now the **Wo Hing Museum;** several 19th-century churches; the 1850s **Old Prison,** also known as Hale Paahao ("stuck-in-irons house"); the docked **Brig**

Carthaginian *(Adm. fee),* whose hold contains a museum of whales and whaling; and the 1859 coral-block **Lahaina Courthouse** on Wharf Street. If you need a break from the heat, have a seat under the sprawling banyan tree planted behind the courthouse in 1873 and now shading almost an acre. Or drop into the 1901 **Pioneer Inn** *(658 Wharf St.),* whose waterfront saloon is Lahaina's social center and whose decor and atmosphere recall the old whaling days.

A series of beaches, most fronted by resort hotels, condominiums, and golf courses, lie north of town along Hawaii 30 in **Kaanapali** and **Kapalua Beach.**

Leaving Lahaina retrace your route south along Hawaii 30 and pick up Hawaii 310 as it edges past **Maalaea Bay,** a popular spot for windsurfing. Passing by **Kealia Pond,** look for endangered Hawaiian black-necked stilts wading in the shallows. Continue south to **Kihei,** a resort area often cited as an example of rampant and haphazard development. On the plus side, the beaches here are long, the water great for boogie boarding and swimming.

Just north of Kihei, turn on Hawaii 311 (Mokulele Highway) as it heads inland across the isthmus that separates the two halves of the island. In ❹ **Puunene** stop at the **Alexander & Baldwin Sugar Museum** *(Hansen Rd.*

Lahaina Historic District

and Puunene Ave. 808-871-8058. Daily July-Aug., closed Sun. Sept.-June; adm. fee) for an explanation of Maui's sugar industry and the ethnic groups that worked the cane fields. A model factory shows how cane is processed.

Jog over to Hawaii 380, turn right on Hawaii 36, and

Molokini

An eroded remnant of a volcano about 100,000 years old and the smallest link in the Hawaiian chain, Molokini lies just 2 miles off the southwest coast of Maui. The islet is shaped like a horseshoe, embracing coral reefs that swarm with sea life: sea urchins with red spines, an octopus dozing on a coral mound, a manta ray with a 10-foot wingspan flapping along gracefully, and schools and schools of rainbow-hued fish. The water around Molokini is a warm 77˚F, with visibility often exceeding 150 feet, making it a popular snorkeling spot. *(For more information, contact the Maui Convention & Visitors Bureau at 808-244-3530.)*

143

proceed to Hawaii 37. After the town of Pukalani take Hawaii 377, which leads to Haleakala Crater Road (Hawaii 378). Now you're in **Kula** (golden meadows), an upcountry area favored by ranchers and flower growers. The road climbs among jacaranda and macadamia trees as it ascends **Haleakala,** a shield volcano that rises 10,023 feet above the sea and drops another 19,000 feet below the sea's surface to the ocean floor. With its middle slopes often in clouds, it floats somewhere between heaven and earth.

After 11 miles the road reaches the headquarters of **5 Haleakala National Park ★ ★** *(808-572-9306. Adm. fee),* set off by subalpine shrubs, mostly yellow-blossomed

Summit of 10,023-foot Puu Ulaulu (Red Hill), Haleakala National Park

mamanes. Look for the nene, the endangered state bird of Hawaii. It's related to a Canada goose that came to Hawaii, and, like many snowbird tourists, decided never to go home. As you continue driving up the volcano's slopes, pause at the overlooks for spectacular views of island and "crater" (technically Haleakala is an erosional depression). Above 9,000 feet the vegetation thins out, exposing cinders and lava. This seemingly harsh habitat nurtures one of the world's rarest plants, the silversword, which resembles a tumbleweed bristling with shining daggers. During its long lifetime—up to 50 years—the plant blooms just once, in a burst of purple flowers.

As you near the summit, stop at the **Haleakala Visitor Center** to see exhibits on the geology and lore of the volcano. The center perches on the rim of the depression, which measures 7.5 miles long, 2.5 miles wide, and 3,000 feet deep— immense enough to plunk Manhattan Island inside with room to spare. To get a feeling of its size and silence, hike a bit down the **Sliding Sands Trail.** You'll see why the terrain is often compared to the moon.

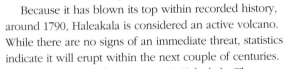
Relaxing, Maui-style

Because it has blown its top within recorded history, around 1790, Haleakala is considered an active volcano. While there are no signs of an immediate threat, statistics indicate it will erupt within the next couple of centuries.

Sunrise is a popular time to visit Haleakala. Then, an incandescent orange stain seeps across the eastern edge of the cold, twilit world. As honey-colored light spills into the crater, your frozen cheeks take in the warmth with primeval gratitude, and you can understand why the ancient islanders worshiped the sun. Because visitors are particularly plentiful at sunrise, some people prefer the more solitary experience of sunset. In either case, bring warm clothes and remember that Madame Pele, the Hawaiian goddess of volcanoes, doesn't appreciate people removing rocks, no matter how tiny. According to Hawaiian belief, removing stones (which have mana, or spiritual power) puts nature out of balance.

Descend from Haleakala to Pukalani and take Hawaii 365 to **Makawao,** a town of Western-style, false-fronted buildings where Maui's heritage of cattle ranching and cowboys blends with the New Age influence of craftspeople and alternative healers.

Drive on to Hawaii 360 and turn right onto the **Hana Highway ★★,** considered the most beautiful coastal drive in the state. At times hugging cliffs above the sea, it weaves past streams, waterfalls, and rain forests spangled by tropical flowers. Don't expect to rush on this road, as it dictates its own pace, creeping around hundreds of curves and crossing dozens of one-lane bridges.

Biking Down

145

Why not join a bike tour down Haleakala? A number of Maui outfitters take riders to the summit by van, dress them in slickers, gloves, and safety helmets (resembling Darth Vader on holiday), and then lead them on a downhill run. The road swoops and zigzags from above 10,000 feet to sea level in some 38 miles. From a realm of barren cinders that looks like the moon, bikers descend through rolling ranch country to fields of pineapple and sugarcane. And don't worry if the only thing you've pedaled lately is a desk chair. Gravity does all the work, while you have all the fun. (For more information contact the Maui Convention & Visitors Bureau 808-244-3530 or 800-525-6284.)

Maui

Past tiny **6** **Kailua** look for rainbow eucalyptus and mountain apple trees, followed by bamboo forests. At the **Waikamoi Ridge Trail** *(Past Milepost 9)* walk through a rain forest where fragrant ginger grows and big-leafed vines climb eucalyptus trees. It's also worth a stop ahead at the **Puohokamoa Falls** for a cooling dip in the pooled waters or a walk among ti plants and ferns. For a broad ocean view, drive on to **Kaumahina State Wayside Park.** From here, the road winds along cliffs to U-shaped **Honomanu Bay,** whose often turbulent surf beats against a black-sand beach. On cliffs above the beach look for the flame-red flowers of African tulip trees.

At the **Keanae Arboretum** *(Past Mile 16)* trails thread among monkeypod, palm, "elephant-ear," plumeria, breadfruit, and papaya trees. At the nearby **Keanae Overlook** *(Past Mile 17)* the view takes in the taro patches and small settlement on the Keanae Peninsula.

Endangered Hawaiian black-necked stilt

Beyond the hamlet of Wailua, you'll find a waterfall at almost every curve in the road. The water is produced by rainfall on the upper slopes of Haleakala, which gets an average of 390 inches annually. Pause at **Puaa Kaa State Wayside Park** *(Past Mile 22)* for a picnic among tree ferns, guavas, and torchlike red gingers; a pretty waterfall here tumbles into a pool. Ten miles farther on **Waianapanapa State Park** *(Turn off past Mile 32. 808-243-5354)* has a black-sand beach and caves that formed from lava tubes.

When you finally arrive in **7** **Hana,** you can celebrate your endurance by buying an "I Survived the Hana Highway" T-shirt. This quiet town lies between emerald hills and blue Hana Bay. The main activities here are cattle ranching and a relaxed style of tourism, launched in 1946 by the **Hotel Hana-Maui** *(808-248-8211),* an elegant, low-key retreat. Near the hotel, the 1838 lava-rock **Wananalua Church** *(808-248-8211)* still stands. Another popular local institution, cluttered **Hasegawa General Store,** has actually had a song written about it. At the **Hana Cultural Center** *(Uakea Rd. 808-248-8622. Donation)* you can see colorful Hawaiian quilts, native shells, and the town's old jail.

Twisting, narrow, sometimes jolting Hawaii 31 heads south out of Hana, still following the coast. After about 8 miles it reaches **Wailua Falls,** a 100-foot cascade framed in greenery like a postcard from paradise. Continue a couple of miles to **Oheo Gulch** *(Near the Haleakala National Park signs).* The gulch and its waterfalls and pools are formed by tumbling Palikea Stream, which begins high on Haleakala and runs to the sea. (As you explore here, be wary of flash floods and slippery rocks.)

Just over a mile away, the tiny village of **Kipahulu** is well known for its small white-frame **Palapala Hoomau Church.** Aviator Charles Lindbergh, who made history with his 1927 solo flight from New York to Paris, is buried in the church's peaceful cemetery overlooking the Pacific.

To return to Kahului, about three hours away, take Hawaii 31 to 360 to 36. Along the way you may spot windsurfers who race at

Papaya trees, Hana Highway

Waianapanapa State Park, off the Hana Highway

incredible speeds in the offshore breezes at **Hookipa Beach Park.** Nearby **Lower Paia,** a former sugar mill town, now boasts a laid-back population of surfers, latter-day hippies, and craftspeople. The drive ends about 9 miles farther on, back in Kahului.

Hawaii★★

● 400 miles ● 4 to 5 days ● Year-round

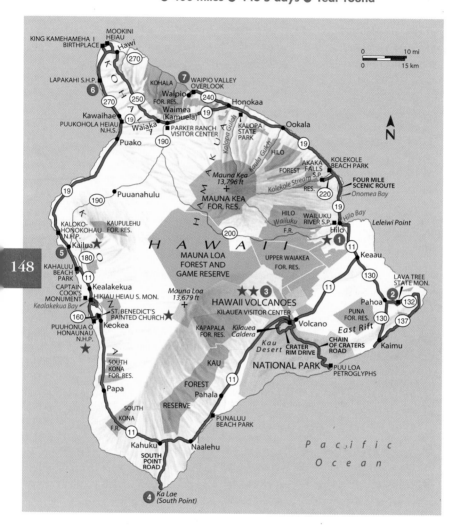

The Big Island, the island of Hawaii, deserves its nickname. More than double the area of all the other Hawaiian islands combined, it's also almost twice the size of Delaware and about 65 times bigger than the Principality of Liechtenstein, and more than 6,000 times the size of Monaco. It happens to be beautiful as well.

This drive roams the edges of the Big Island, beginning in the garden town of Hilo then traveling through the island's extensive volcanic zone. It makes a side trip to the southernmost point in the United States before

percolating through Kona coffee country. After basking in
the sunshine resort areas of Kailua and Kohala, you can
take a look at ancient temples before making your way
through lush coastal rain forests back to Hilo.

❶ Hilo★ *(Convention & Visitors Bureau, 250 Keawe St.
808-961-5797)* has the weathered look of a South Pacific
outpost, perhaps because it receives 137 inches of rain a
year. Its warm, moist climate suits the orchids and other
tropical plants that are grown commercially throughout
the region. (The Visitors Bureau can direct you to gardens and nurseries.)

A natural garden spot, **Rainbow Falls** *(Off Waianuenue
Ave. in Wailuku River State Park)* is formed as the Wailuku

149

Rainbow Falls in Wailuku River State Park, Hilo

River plunges 80 feet and raises mists that sunlight trans-
figures into rainbows, especially in the morning.

Hilo's **Lyman House Memorial Museum★** *(276 Haili
St. 808-935-5021. Mon.-Sat.; adm. fee)* displays such Hawaiiana as a thatched house; minerals, including lava; and
ethnic artifacts, like a canoe breaker—a stone tied to a
rope, which was thrown into an enemy canoe. The 1839
Mission House next door was built by Congregationalist
missionaries, which accounts for its New England style.
Family items include quilts, furniture, and the preserved

Hilo sunrise

Hilo Orchids

An orchid lei settles lightly on your shoulders with the island spirit of *aloha*—friendliness and goodwill. Many orchids come from Hilo, whose warm climate and 137 inches of annual rainfall offer perfect growing conditions. Because orchids look so natural in Hawaii, it's surprising that almost all were originally imported from tropical Asia and South America. Hilo's industry took hold in the 1940s with backyard gardeners, mainly Japanese and Filipinos, who began cultivating orchids as a small cash crop. There are more than 25,000 orchid species and at least 100,000 hybrids.

New England autumn leaves that Mrs. Lyman poignantly showed her children, who lived in a tropical world without a fall season.

In 1946 and 1960 tsunamis wiped out much of the waterfront along Hilo Bay, so you see parks here instead of businesses. **Banyan Drive** is lined with banyan trees (of course), some planted by celebrities such as aviator Amelia Earhart. On the west side stand the Japanese bridges and stone lanterns of **Liliuokalani Gardens.** Any morning except Sunday, you can get a good sense of the island's mix of humanity when the day's catch is auctioned off in pidgin at the **Suisan Fish Market** *(By Suisan retail shop, near Lihiwai St. 7:30 a.m.).*

From Hilo head south on Hawaii 11. To explore a kingdom of lava and black-sand beaches, make a side trip to the sparsely settled eastern corner of the island. At Keaau turn onto Hawaii 130 to Pahoa. Property is relatively cheap around here, as you'd expect in an area where housing developments are periodically buried under molten lava.

Take Hawaii 132 and drive through a tropical forest thick with vines and impatiens to ❷ **Lava Tree State Monument.** A grove of ohia trees grew here until about 1790, when lava from the east rift of Kilauea encased the trunks and left rigid shells standing 12 feet tall. The former forest floor now looks like crumpled asphalt.

Turn right onto Hawaii 137 and follow the shoreline. Among the hala trees, hidden houses belong to the sort of people who enjoy living in a remote place. One pleasant young hitchhiker, scented with patchouli, introduced himself as Brother ("the name just feels right") and discussed the wheat meatloaf recipe he hoped to "sell to some big company and make a fortune." If you want to swim here, ask locals about beach areas and water safety.

Hawaii 137 ends where molten lava buried the town of Kalapana in 1990. Take Hawaii 130 north to Hawaii 11 and proceed southwest.

Volcanic activity has defined the character of the island for centuries, and at ❸ **Hawaii Volcanoes National Park ★ ★** *(808-967-7311, eruption update 808-967-7977. Adm. fee)* you'll see the newest earth on earth. The east rift of **Kilauea** has been pouring lava since 1983. Also in the park rises 13,679-foot **Mauna Loa,** a volcano of such bulk that California's entire Sierra Nevada range could fit comfortably inside. Both are shield volcanoes, the kind that build up through countless small eruptions, in contrast to explosive types like Mount St. Helens.

Take the 20-mile-long **Chain of Craters Road** that passes through a cooled lava flow (1969-1974) so profuse it could literally pave a highway around the globe. This is a good place for a lava lesson: the jagged kind is called *aa,* while *pahoehoe* is the smooth, ropy variety. Around Mile 17, a 1-mile trail leads through the **Puu Loa Petroglyphs,** a field of more than 15,000 images and figures carved in lava by earlier Hawaiians. The road ends abruptly where lava covers it like tar on a roof. Across the crinkly surface park rangers mark a path to a viewpoint close to current flows; check with rangers for safety tips. The temperature of flowing lava is about 2100°F. When it hits the ocean, steam boils up, and the air fills with roaring, snapping noises.

Along the 11-mile **Crater Rim Drive** you can explore the margin of the Kilauea Caldera. Start by learning about volcanoes through the film and exhibits at the **Kilauea Visitor Center.** Then take the short **Earthquake Trail** (near the Volcano House hotel) to look at the nearly 2-mile-wide **Kilauea Caldera.** Drive on clockwise around the rim and enter a rain forest of ferns and ohia trees with scarlet flowers. Stop to see **Kilauea Iki Crater,** once a lake of seething lava formed by a fountain shooting nearly 2,000 feet high during the powerful 1959 eruption. Be sure to explore the rambling **Thurston Lava Tube,** formed during an eruption hundreds of years ago. The volcano goddess, Pele, is said to live in the steaming precincts of the **Halemaumau Crater,** and local

Along Banyan Drive, Hilo

people make offerings of native Hawaiian song and dance for her at the crater's edge. Beyond this stretches a strange, barren landscape—the **Kau Desert,** produced by the acid rain that is a by-product of the island's volcanism.

Farther along at the **Jaggar Museum,** you can become a connoisseur of lava, from Pele's tears (volcanic glass) to volcanic bombs. Drive on to see the steam vents (or fumaroles) of appropriately named **Steaming Bluff,** and **Sulfur Banks,** whose smelly volcanic gases have tinted the rocks in rust

Puu Oo spewing molten lava

and yellowish-green. The loop ends back at the Visitor Center.

Continue southwest on Hawaii 11, where a short detour leads to the well-known, black-sand **Punaluu Beach Park.** Farther on, you reach the southernmost town in the United States, **Naalehu,** where monkeypod trees form a green canopy over the road. About 6 miles past Naalehu an 11-mile-long side road takes you through bare country to ❹ **Ka Lae (South Point),** the nation's southernmost spot. At road's end you're 500 miles farther south than Miami. Along the windy coast here you'll find the ruins of a stone *heiau* (temple) and a fishing shrine.

Just after you rejoin Hawaii 11 west, you'll see the vast 1868 lava flow that came from Mauna Loa to the north. Winding into the South Kona area, the drive turns onto Hawaii 160. On the way downhill take a brief side trip to **St. Benedict's Painted Church ★,** whose ornate interior was created between 1899 and 1904 by a Belgian priest using ordinary house paint. The church's inside posts look like palm trees, with fronds spreading across sunset skies. Panels showing biblical scenes were used to teach Christian themes to Hawaiians who couldn't read.

Continue on Hawaii 160 to **Puuhonua o Honaunau National Historical Park ★** *(808-328-2288. Adm. fee),* dating from the 16th century. A "place of refuge," this was where Hawaiians who had violated one of the many *kapu* (taboos) sought a safe haven. If they could reach here before being captured, they could avoid punishment or death. On the park's seaside grounds stand a rebuilt temple with wooden statues and a stone wall that separated refuges from the adjoining royal palace area, now in ruins.

North about 4 miles lies **Kealakekua Bay,** a marine preserve popular with snorkelers and a site that changed Hawaiian history. Here in 1779 the two

Fern in Kilauea Crater

ships of Capt. James Cook appeared under full sail—fulfilling a Hawaiian prophecy that the god Lono would return to earth on a "floating island," with banners of white tapa. Cook was welcomed as Lono but later was killed during an altercation. The **Hikiau Heiau State Monument** is a temple devoted to Lono. **Captain Cook's Monument** stands on the far side of the bay.

Take Middle Keei and Napoopoo Roads to return to Hawaii 11 and head north. After 9 miles you can turn off to **Kahaluu Beach Park.** Here the snorkeling is easy, but stay in the gentle water close to shore.

Continue to ❺ **Kailua ★** *(Convention & Visitors Bureau, 75-5719 Alii Dr. 808-329-7787),* a deep-sea fishing and coffee-growing capital, and a sunny resort region. Even Hawaiian monarchs liked it here, and Kamehameha the Great spent his last years in the early 1800s at **Ahuena Heiau** *(Grounds of King Kamehameha Kona Beach Hotel, 75-5660 Palani Rd. 808-329-2911),* cogitating on proper government. A prayer tower and wooden images have been reconstructed on the temple site.

Hawaiian royalty summered at **Hulihee Palace** *(75-5718 Alii Dr. 808-329-1877. Adm. fee),* a harborside structure built in 1838 of lava and coral. Rooms feature the belongings of Hawaiian monarchs, including the furniture of King Kalakua and the spears of Kamehameha the Great.

153

Roadside waterfall near Honomu

Built in the 1830s, **Mokuaikaua Church** *(Across from Hulihee Palace. 808-329-1589)* reflects the New England heritage of the island's Boston missionaries, though it is built of island materials—lava rock with coral-based mortar—and filled with koa-wood pews. It is said to be the oldest church in the state.

After leaving Kailua on Hawaii 19, stop to visit the ruins of an old native village at **Kaloko-Honokohau National Historical Park** *(3 miles N, call for directions. 808-329-6881).* Legend says the bones of Kamehameha the Great are buried nearby. Soon you enter the hot, dry coastline of South Kohala. The area here is dotted with luxury resorts, of which the **Hilton Waikoloa Village** *(Mile 76. 808-885-1234 or 800-228-9000)* ranks as the supreme fantasy. The

Kona Coffee

Only one state in the U.S. grows coffee—Hawaii— and the best comes from the Kona district of the Big Island. In fact, conoisseurs rank this arabica coffee among the world's top brews. A missionary planted the first trees in Kona around 1828. The growing conditions were perfect—rich volcanic soil, an elevation above 1,200 feet, cool breezes, light rains. In springtime, slopes are blanketed with white blossoms, aptly named Kona Snow. Between September and January, field workers harvest cherry red berries. Coffee's valuable part is its seed—the coffee bean. Each year, a tree produces only enough beans to make a single pound of roasted coffee. But brewed up, that coffee is as pure and intoxicating as sunshine.

development has created its own canal, beach, waterfalls, and private dolphin lagoon. Canalboats and trams ferry guests around the enormous complex.

In **Puako,** the **Puako Petroglyphs Archaeological Preserve** *(Via Mauna Lani and N. Kaniku Drs. to Holoholokai Beach Park; 0.8-mile trail begins in parking lot)* protects 3,000 lava carvings of unknown age and indeterminate meaning. The images include stick figures, triangular torsos, and what may be columns of warriors marching with their chiefs.

Continue north on Hawaii 19, and just before you reach Kawaihae, stop at **Puukohola Heiau National Historic Site** *(808-882-7218).* In 1790, the 7-foot-tall Kamehameha the Great built a temple to his war god here, as a prophet said he must in order to conquer the Hawaiian archipelago. Human sacrifices took place on the lava-rock platform at the site.

From the town of Kawaihae, Hawaii 270 follows the coast 12 miles north to ❻ **Lapakahi State Historical Park** *(808-974-6200),* which preserves a remnant fishing village founded around 1300. On a pretty piece of shoreline you'll see a canoe house, stone fishing god, partially restored residences, and Hawaiian board games.

At Mile 20 turn off to Upolu Airport, go 2 miles and take a left on a dirt road. After 2 more miles, you'll reach the remote and haunting **Mookini Heiau,** used for human sacrifices. It's said warriors passed rocks along a 14-mile human chain to build the 250-foot-long structure. Nearby stands a large lava-rock enclosure marking the 1758 **King Kamehameha I Birthplace.**

As you round the northwest tip of the island, turn off Hawaii 270 onto Hawaii 250, which takes you to Waimea (Kamuela). At the **Parker Ranch Visitors Center** *(Hawaii 19. 808-885-7655. Adm. fee)* you can learn about one of the nation's biggest ranches (225,000 acres), founded in 1847. Off Hawaii 190, the ranch's historic houses can be visited—the elegant **Puuopelu** *(Adm. fee),* with French Regency furnishings; and **Mana Hale** *(Adm. fee),* a simple 1840s New England saltbox built by ranch founder John Palmer Parker.

Follow Hawaii 19 to Honokaa, a former sugar mill town, and turn left on Hawaii 240 for 9 miles to the ❼ **Waipio Valley Overlook.** Before

you, cliffs rise as high as 2,000 feet to guard a valley of taro patches; fishponds; and coconut, guava, and banana trees. Hawaiians have lived in this valley for a thousand years, though a tsunami in 1946 drove out most of the population. On certain nights the nobility of old are said to return here and light up the valley with their torch marches. A steep dirt road requiring four-wheel-drive or foot power leads down to the valley; or you can take the hourly Waipio Valley shuttle van *(808-775-7121. Mon.-Fri.; fare).*

Return to Hawaii 19 and head south down the **Hamakua Coast,** a region of lush greenery and streams. You can wander in a rain forest on the lower slopes of Mauna Kea volcano at **Kalopa State Park** *(808-974-6200),* then drive on to the black-sand beach at **Kolekole Beach Park.** The surf here is treacherous, but Kolekole Stream has pools to splash in.

Turn inland on Hawaii 220 for a short side trip to the 420-foot-high cascade at **Akaka Falls State Park** *(808-974-6200),* located along a trail lush with tropical plants. For more of the rain forest take the Four Mile Scenic Route and make a stop at the **Hawaii Tropical Botanical Garden** *(808-964-5233. Adm. fee);* along the way you'll be treated to glimpses of Onomea Bay. Return to Hilo on Hawaii 19, enjoying the view of Hilo Bay.

Puuhonua o Honaunau National Historical Park, South Kona

National Park Service Information for California, Nevada, and Hawaii National Parks *415-556-0560.*

CALIFORNIA
California Division of Tourism General information *916-322-2881 or 916-322-1396.*
Department of Parks and Recreation General information *916-653-6995.* Camping reservations *800-444-7275.*
Department of Transportation Road Conditions *916-445-1534.*
Dept. of Fish and Game General information *916-653-7664.* Fishing information *800-ASK-FISH.* Hunting information *916-227-2244.*

NEVADA
Nevada Commission on Tourism General information *775-687-4322.*
Division of State Parks General information *775-687-4384.*
Department of Transportation Road Conditions *775-793-1313* (northern Nev.). *702-593-4021* (southern Nev.). 702-738-8888 (eastern Nev.). *775-623-1313* (northcentral Nev.).
Division of Wildlife Hunting and fishing information *775-688-1500.*

HAWAII
OAHU
Oahu Convention & Visitors Bureau *808-923-1811.*
Division of Aquatic Resources Fishing license information *808-587-0100.*
Division of Forestry and Wildlife Hunting information *808-587-0166.*
Division of State Parks General information *808-587-0300.*
KAUAI
Kauai Convention & Visitors Bureau *808-245-3971.*
Division of Aquatic Resources Fishing license information *808-274-3344.*
Division of Forestry and Wildlife Hunting information *808-274-3433.*
Division of State Parks General information *808-274-3444.*
MAUI
Maui Convention & Visitors Bureau *808-244-3530.*
Division of Aquatic Resources Fishing license information *808-243-5294.*
Division of Forestry and Wildlife Hunting information *808-984-8100.*
Division of State Parks General information *808-984-8109.*
HAWAII
Hawaii Convention & Visitors Bureau *808-961-5797.*
Division of Aquatic Resources Fishing license information *808-974-6201.*
Division of Forestry and Wildlife Hunting information *808-933-4221.*
Division of State Parks General information *808-974-6200.*

156

HOTEL & MOTEL CHAINS
(Accommodations in all three states unless otherwise noted)

Best Western International *800-528-1234*
Choice Hotels *800-4-CHOICE*
Clarion Hotels *800-CLARION*
Comfort Inns *800-228-5150*
Courtyard by Marriott *800-321-2211*
Days Inn *800-325-2525* (except Hawaii)
Econo Lodge *800-446-6900* (except Hawaii)
Embassy Suites *800-EMBASSY* (except Nev.)
Fairfield Inn by Marriott *800-228-2800*
Hilton Hotels *800-HILTONS*
Holiday Inns *800-HOLIDAY*
Howard Johnson *800-654-2000*
Hyatt Hotels and Resorts *800-233-1234*
Marriott Hotels Resorts Suites *800-228-9290*
Motel Six *800-466-8356* (except Hawaii)
Quality Inns-Hotels-Suites *800-228-5151*
Radisson Hotels International *800-333-3333* (except Hawaii and Nev.)
Ramada Inns *800-2-RAMADA* (except Hawaii)
Red Lion Hotels Inc. *800-547-8010* (except Hawaii)
Red Roof Inns *800-843-7663* (Calif. only)
Ritz Carlton *800-241-3333* (except Nev.)
Sheraton Hotels & Inns *800-325-3535*
Super 8 Motels *800-843-1991* (except Hawaii)
Vagabond Inns *800-522-1555* (except Hawaii)
Westin Hotels and Resorts *800-228-3000* (except Nev.)

ILLUSTRATIONS CREDITS
Photographs in this book are by Phil Schermeister, except the following: 25 Jeff Gnass; 65 (lower) Robert Landau/Westlight; 69 O. Louis Mazzatenta; 77 Kevin S. Schumacher; 91 Steve Raymer; 92 Michael S. Yamashita; 93 Craig Aurness; 116 (upper) David Muench; 136 Jeff Gnass; 146 Chris Johns, National Geographic photographer; 152 (upper) James A. Sugar.

NOTES ON AUTHOR AND PHOTOGRAPHER
JERRY CAMARILLO DUNN, JR., is that rare phenomenon—a native Californian. Winner of three Lowell Thomas Awards from the Society of American Travel Writers, he is a contributing editor at National Geographic TRAVELER. He also writes for National Geographic WORLD and has contributed to several Society books. Among Jerry's other works are *The Smithsonian Guide to Historic America: The Rocky Mountain States; Tricks of the Trade;* and *Idiom Savant: Slang As It Is Slung.* He lives with his wife, Merry, and sons, Graham and Lachlan, in Ojai, California. This book is dedicated to his father, who loved California.

For the past 20 years, PHIL SCHERMEISTER has worked as both a photojournalist and travel photographer on assignments around the United States. His work appears regularly in travel publications including National Geographic's TRAVELER magazine. He and his wife make their home in San Francisco.

*A*hwahnee Hotel, Yosemite N.P., Calif. 88
Akaka Falls S.P., Hawaii 155
Alcatraz Island, Calif. 42, 43
Alexander & Baldwin Sugar Museum, Puunene, Maui, Hawaii 143
Ancient Bristlecone Pine Forest, Calif. 91-92
Anderson Valley, Calif. 31
Angeles Crest Highway, Calif. 71
Angels Camp, Calif. 100-101
Anini Beach Park, Kauai, Hawaii 135
Anza-Borrego Desert S.P., Calif. 76, 80, 81
Arboretum of Los Angeles County, Arcadia, Calif. 70
Arcata, Calif. 11-12
Arrowhead, Lake, Calif. 64, 71
Asian Art Museum of San Francisco, Calif. 44
Auburn, Calif. 105
Audubon Canyon Ranch, Calif. 34-35
Autry Museum of Western Heritage, Los Angeles, Calif. 67
Avalon, Catalina Island, Calif. 74

*B*alboa Island, Calif. 75
Balboa Park, San Diego, Calif. 78
Benicia, Calif. 47-48
Beverly Hills, Los Angeles, Calif. 64, 67-68
Big Bear Lake, Calif. 64, 71
Big Sur, Calif. 50, 53-54
Bishop Museum, Honolulu, Hawaii 128
Bodie S.H.P., Calif. 86, 90
Bolsa Chica Ecological Reserve, Calif. 74
Boonville, Calif. 30, 31
Boulder City/Hoover Dam Museum, Boulder City, Nev. 123

*C*abrillo N.M., Calif. 77
California Academy of Sciences, San Francisco, Calif. 44-45
California Palace of the Legion of Honor, San Francisco, Calif. 44
California State Indian Museum, Sacramento, Calif. 98
Calistoga, Calif. 37-38
Calaveras Big Trees S.P., Calif. 101
Cambria, Calif. 50, 52
Carlin, Nev. 115
Carmel-by-the-Sea, Calif. 55
Carson City, Nev. 106, 109-110
Carson Mansion, Eureka, Calif. 11
Castle Crags S.P., Calif. 18, 21
Catalina Island, Calif. 74
Cave Lake S.P., Nev. 117
Channel Islands N.P., Calif. 63
Chinatown, San Francisco, Calif. 42
Chumash Painted Cave S.H.P., Calif. 62
Coloma, Calif. 98-99
Columbia S.H.P., Calif. 101
Coronado, Calif. 79

D.L. Bliss S.P., Calif. 102-103
Dante's View, Death Valley, Calif. 93
Death Valley N.P., Calif. 86, 92-93
Del Norte Coast Redwoods S.P., Calif. 13
Devils Postpile N.M., Calif. 91
Diamond Head, Oahu, Hawaii 126
Disneyland, Anaheim, Calif. 72-73
Donner Memorial S.P., Calif. 103
Downieville, Calif. 104

*E*agle and High Peak Mines, Julian, Calif. 80
El Capitan, Yosemite N.P., Calif. 88
Elko, Nev. 115
Ely, Nev. 113
Emerald Bay, Lake Tahoe, Calif. 102
Empire Mine S.H.P., Calif. 105

Encinitas, Calif. 84
Eureka, Calif. 10, 11
Eureka, Nev. 113, 114
Exploratorium, San Francisco, Calif. 43

*F*armers Market, Los Angeles, Calif. 66
Ferndale, Calif. 10, 17
Fisherman's Wharf, San Francisco, Calif. 40, 42
Forest Lawn Memorial Park, Glendale, Calif. 69, 70
Fort Bragg, Calif. 30
Fort Humboldt S.H.P., Eureka, Calif. 11
Fort Jones, Calif. 15-16
Fort Ross S.H.P., Calif. 27-28
Fresno, Calif. 87
Furnace Creek, Calif. 93

*G*amble House, Pasadena, Calif. 70
Genoa, Nev. 106, 109
Ghirardelli Square, San Francisco, Calif. 42
Glacier Point, Yosemite N.P., Calif. 87
Gold Canyon, Nev. 110
Golden Gate Bridge, San Francisco, Calif. 32-33, 44
Golden Gate Park, San Francisco, Calif. 44
Great Basin N.P., Nev. 113, 117
Grizzly Creek Redwoods S.P., Calif. 17

*H*aleakala N.P., Maui, Hawaii 140, 144-145
Half Dome (peak), Yosemite N.P., Calif. 88
Hana, Maui, Hawaii 146
Hana Highway, Maui, Hawaii 140, 145-146
Hanalei, Kauai, Hawaii 135-136
Hanalei Valley Lookout, Kauai, Hawaii 135
Hanauma Bay State Underwater Park, Oahu, Hawaii 131
Happy Camp, Calif. 14
Hawaii Maritime Center,

Honolulu, Hawaii 127
Hawaii Volcanoes N.P.,
  Hawaii 150-152
Hearst Castle, San Simeon,
  Calif. 50, 53
Hilo, Hawaii 149-150
Hollywood, Los Angeles,
  Calif. 64, 67
Honolulu, Hawaii 124-128
Honolulu Academy of Arts,
  Honolulu, Hawaii 126
Honomanu Bay,
  Maui, Hawaii 146
Hookipa Beach Park,
  Maui, Hawaii 147
Hoover Dam, Nev.-Ariz. 118,
  122-123
Huleia Stream, Kauai, Hawaii
  133
Humboldt Lagoons S.P.,
  Calif. 12
Humboldt State
  University Natural
  History Museum,
  Arcata, Calif. 11-12
Huntington Beach, Calif. 74
Huntington Library, Art Col-
  lections and Botanical Gar-
  dens, San Marino, Calif. 70

Iao Valley S.P., Maui, Hawaii
  141
Imperial Palace Auto Collec-
  tion, Las Vegas, Nev. 120-121
Indian Canyons, Palm
  Springs, Calif. 82-83
Indian Grinding Rock S.H.P.,
  Calif. 100
Indio, Calif. 81
International Market Place,
  Honolulu, Hawaii 125
Iolani Palace, Honolulu,
  Hawaii 126-127

J. Paul Getty Museum, near
  Malibu, Calif. 68-69
Jackson, Calif. 100
Jedediah Smith Redwoods
  S.P., Calif. 14
John Muir N.H.S., Martinez,
  Calif. 47
Joshua Tree N.P., Calif. 76,
  81-82
Julian, Calif. 80

Kahaluu Beach Park, Hawaii
  153
Kahului, Maui, Hawaii 140-
  141
Kailua, Hawaii 153
Kalalau Lookout, Kauai,
  Hawaii 139
Kalalau Trail, Kauai, Hawaii
  136
Kaloko-Honokohau N.H.P.,
  Hawaii 153
Kalopa S.P., Hawaii 155
Kanaha Pond Wildlife Sanctu-
  ary, Maui, Hawaii 141
Kaumahina State Wayside
  Park, Maui, Hawaii 146
Kealakekua Bay, Hawaii
  152-153
Kepaniwai Park, Maui,
  Hawaii 141
Kihei, Maui, Hawaii 143
Kilauea Point N.W.R., Kauai,
  Hawaii 135
Kilauea Visitor Center, Hawaii
  Volcanoes N.P., Hawaii 151
Kings Canyon N.P., Calif. 86,
  94, 95
Kokee S.P., Kauai, Hawaii
  138
Kruse Rhododendron S.R.,
  Calif. 28

La Jolla, Calif. 76, 85
La Purísima Mission S.H.P.,
  Calif. 61
Laguna Art Museum of the
  Orange County Museum of
  Art, Laguna Beach, Calif. 75
Laguna Beach, Calif. 75
Lahaina, Maui, Hawaii 140,
  142-143
Lake Mead National Recre-
  ation Area, Nev. 118, 122
Lake Tahoe Nevada S.P.,
  Nev. 108
Lamoille Canyon Scenic Area,
  Nev. 116
Lapakahi S.H.P., Hawaii 154
Las Vegas, Nev. 118-121
Las Vegas Natural History
  Museum, Las Vegas, Nev.
  119
Lassen Volcanic N.P., Calif.
  18, 24-25
Lava Tree S.M., Hawaii 150

Lehman Caves, Nev. 117
Liberace Museum, Las Vegas,
  Nev. 121
Lihue, Kauai, Hawaii 132, 133
Living Desert Wildlife and
  Botanical Park, Palm Desert,
  Calif. 82
Long Beach, Calif.: *Queen
  Mary* (ocean liner) 73-74
Los Angeles, Calif. 64-68
Los Angeles County Museum
  of Art, Los Angeles, Calif. 66
Los Angeles Zoo, Los Ange-
  les, Calif. 67
Lost City Museum, Overton,
  Nev. 122
Lumahai Beach, Kauai,
  Hawaii 136
Luther Burbank Home & Gar-
  dens, Santa Rosa, Calif. 27
Lydgate Park, Kauai, Hawaii
  134

M. H. de Young Memorial
  Museum, San Francisco,
  Calif. 44
Makawao, Maui, Hawaii 145
Malakoff Diggins S.H.P.,
  Calif. 104-105
Malibu, Calif. 68-69
Mammoth Lakes (resort area),
  Calif. 86, 90
Mann's Chinese Theatre, Los
  Angeles, Calif. 67
Manzanar N.H.S., Calif. 92
Marble Mountain Wilderness,
  Calif. 16
Mariposa Grove, Yosemite
  N.P., Calif. 87
Marjorie Barrick Museum of
  Natural History, Las Vegas,
  Nev. 121
Marshall Gold Discovery
  S.H.P., Coloma, Calif. 98-99
Mauna Loa (volcano), Hawaii
  151
McArthur-Burney Falls
  Memorial S.P., Calif. 23
McCloud, Calif. 22-23
Mendocino, Calif. 26, 28-29
Mendocino Headlands S.P.,
  Calif. 29
Mill Valley, Calif. 39
Mission Basilica San Diego
  de Alcalá, San Diego,

Calif. 77
Mission Houses Museum, Honolulu, Hawaii 126
Mission San Carlos Borromeo de Carmelo, Calif. 55
Mission San Juan Capistrano, Calif. 75
Mission San Luis Rey de Francía, San Luis Rey, Calif. 84
Mission Sánta Barbara, Santa Barbara, Calif. 58-59
Mokuaikaua Church, Kailua, Hawaii 153
Molokini (island), Hawaii 143
Mono Lake, Calif. 89
Montecito, Calif. 62
Monterey, Calif. 50, 56-57
Monterey Bay Aquarium, Monterey, Calif. 56
Monterey S.H.P., Monterey, Calif. 56-57
Mookini Heiau, Hawaii 154
Moorten Botanical Garden, Palm Springs, Calif. 83
Mormon Station S.P., Genoa, Nev. 109
Morro Bay, Calif. 52
Mount Diablo S.P., Calif. 47
Mt. Shasta city, Calif. 18, 21
Muir Woods N.M., Calif. 33-34
Murphys Historic Hotel and Lodge, Murphys, Calif. 101
Museum of Contemporary Art, Los Angeles, Calif. 65
Museum of Tolerance, Los Angeles, Calif. 68

*N*BC Studios, Burbank, Calif. 69
Na Pali Coast, Kauai, Hawaii 132, 136
Naalehu, Hawaii 152
Napa Valley, Calif. 37
National Automobile Museum, Reno, Nev. 107
Natural Bridges State Beach, Calif. 57
Natural History Museum of Los Angeles County, Los Angeles, Calif. 65-66
Nevada City, Calif. 105
Nevada Gambling Museum, Virginia City, Nev. 111
Nevada Northern Railway

Museum, Ely, Nev. 113
Nevada State Museum, Carson City, Nev. 110
Newport Beach, Calif. 74-75
Norton Simon Museum, Pasadena, Calif. 70
Nuuanu Pali Lookout, Oahu, Hawaii 130

*O*akland Museum of California, Oakland, Calif. 49
Ojai, Calif. 63
Old Las Vegas Mormon Fort S.H.P., Las Vegas, Nev. 119
Old Town San Diego S.H.P., Calif. 77

*P*acific Grove, Calif. 53, 55-56
Palace of Fine Arts, San Francisco, Calif. 43
Palm Springs, Calif. 76, 82-83
Palm Springs Desert Museum, Palm Springs, Calif. 83
Palomar Observatory, Calif. 84
Parker Ranch Visitors Center, Hawaii 154
Pasadena, Calif. 64, 69-70
Patrick's Point S.P., Calif. 12
Pearl Harbor, Oahu, Hawaii 128-129
Petaluma, Calif. 35-36
Petersen Automotive Museum, Los Angeles, Calif. 66
Pfeiffer Beach, Calif. 54
Pfeiffer Big Sur S.P., Calif. 54
Pioneer Inn, Lahaina, Maui, Hawaii 143
Plumas-Eureka S.P., Calif. 103-104
Point Lobos S.R., Calif. 54-55
Point Reyes N.S., Calif. 35
Poipu Beach Park, Kauai, Hawaii 137
Poipu, Kauai, Hawaii 137
Polynesian Cultural Center, Oahu, Hawaii 130
Prairie Creek Redwoods S.P., Calif. 13
Puaa Kaa State Wayside Park, Maui, Hawaii 146
Puako Petroglyphs Archaeological Preserve, Hawaii 154

Punaluu Beach Park, Hawaii 152
Puu O Kila Lookout, Kauai, Hawaii 139
Puu O Mahuka Heiau S.M., Oahu, Hawaii 129
Puuhonua o Honaunau N.H.P., Hawaii 152
Puukohola Heiau N.H.S., Hawaii 154
Pyramid Lake, Nev. 106, 111

*R*ainbow Falls, Wailuku River S.P., Hilo, Hawaii 149
Red Bluff, Calif. 18, 19
Red Rock Canyon National Conservation Area, Nev. 118, 123
Redwood N.P., Calif. 12-14
Reno, Nev. 106-108
Rim of the World Scenic Byway, Calif. 71
Romano Gabriel Sculpture Garden, Eureka, Calif. 11
Rosicrucian Egyptian Museum and Planetarium, San Jose, Calif. 46
Ruby Mountains, Nev. 115

*S*acramento, Calif. 97-98
Sacred Falls S.P., Oahu, Hawaii 130
Salt Point S.P., Calif. 28
Salton Sea N.W.R., Calif. 81
San Andreas Fault, Calif. 35, 71
San Diego, Calif. 76-79
San Diego Maritime Museum, San Diego, Calif. 79
San Diego Zoo, San Diego, Calif. 78-79
San Francisco, Calif. 40-45
San Francisco Maritime N.H.P., San Francisco, Calif. 42
San Jose, Calif. 40, 45-46
San Luis Obispo, Calif. 51
Santa Barbara, Calif. 58-60
Santa Cruz, Calif. 50, 57
Santa Cruz Mission S.H.P., Calif. 57
Santa Monica, Calif. 68
Santa Rosa, Calif. 26-27

Index

Santa Ynez Valley, Calif. 58, 62

Sausalito, Calif. 33

Scotty's Castle, Death Valley, Calif. 93

Sea Life Park, Oahu, Hawaii 130-131

Sea World, San Diego, Calif. 78

Sequoia N.P., Calif. 86, 94-95

Seventeen Mile Drive, Monterey Peninsula, Calif. 55

Shasta Dam, Calif. 19-20

Shasta Lake, Calif. 18, 20

Shasta, Mount, Calif. 18, 21-22, 23

Shasta S.H.P., Calif. 19

Sierra County Historical Park and Museum at the Kentucky Mine, Calif. 104

Silver Strand State Beach, Calif. 79

Solvang, Calif. 61-62

Sonoma, Calif. 36

Sonoma Coast State Beach, Calif. 27

Sonoma S.H.P., Calif. 36

Southwest Museum, Los Angeles, Calif. 65

Spring Mountain Ranch S.P., Nev. 123

Stinson Beach, Calif. 34

Sugar Pine Point S.P., Calif. 103

Sunset Beach, Oahu, Hawaii 129

Sutter Creek, Calif. 100

Sutter's Fort S.H.P., Sacramento, Calif. 98

Tahoe City, Calif. 103

Tahoe, Lake, Calif.-Nev. 102, 106, 108

Tall Trees Grove, Redwood N.P., Calif. 13

Thurston Lava Tube, Hawaii Volcanoes N.P., Hawaii 151

Torrey Pines S.R., Calif. 84-85

Trinity Alps Wilderness, Calif. 16

Tuolumne Meadows, Yosemite N.P., Calif. 88-89

Union Square, San Francisco, Calif. 41

Universal Studios Hollywood, Universal City, Calif. 69

University of California at Berkeley 48

U.S.S. *Arizona* Memorial, Pearl Harbor, Honolulu, Hawaii 128

Valley of Fire S.P., Nev. 118, 121

Venice, Calif. 68

Ventura, Calif. 62-63

Virginia City, Nev. 106, 109, 110-111

Waialeale, Mount, Kauai, Hawaii 134

Waianapanapa S.P., Maui, Hawaii 146

Waikamoi Ridge Trail, Maui, Hawaii 146

Waikiki Beach, Honolulu, Hawaii 125

Wailua Falls, Kauai, Hawaii 133-134

Wailua Falls, Maui, Hawaii 146-147

Wailua River, Kauai, Hawaii 134

Wailuku, Maui, Hawaii 141

Waimea Bay Beach Park, Oahu, Hawaii 129

Waimea Canyon S.P., Kauai, Hawaii 138

Waimea Falls Park, Oahu, Hawaii 129

Waipio Valley Overlook, Hawaii 154-155

Ward Charcoal Ovens S.H.S., Nev. 116-117

Warner Bros. Studios, Burbank, Calif. 69

Weaverville, Calif. 16-17

Wheeler Peak Scenic Drive, Nev. 117

White Domes, Nev. 122

Whitney, Mount, Calif. 86, 92

William B. Ide Adobe S.H.P., Calif. 19

Winchester Mystery House, San Jose, Calif. 45-46

Yosemite N.P., Calif. 86, 87-88

Yosemite Valley, Calif. 87

Yreka, Calif. 15

160

Composition for this book by the National Geographic Society Book Division. Printed and bound by R.R. Donnelly & Sons, Willard, Ohio. Color separations by Digital Color Image, Pensauken, New Jersey. Paper by Consolidated/Alling & Cory, Willow Grove, Pennsylvania. Cover printed by Miken Companies, Inc. Cheektowaga, New York.

Dunn, Jerry Camarillo.
   National Geographic's driving guides to America. California and Nevada and Hawaii / by Jerry Camarillo Dunn, Jr. ; photographed by Phil Schermeister ; prepared by the Book Division, National Geographic Society.
      p. cm.
   Includes index.
   ISBN 0-7922-3427-8
   1. California—Tours. 2. Nevada—Tours. 3. Hawaii—Tours.
4. Automobile travel—California—Guidebooks. 5. Automobile travel—Nevada—Guidebooks. 6. Automobile travel—Hawaii—Guidebooks.
I. Schermeister, Phil. II. National Geographic Society (U.S.).
Book Division. III. Title.
   F859.3.D76 1996
917.9—dc21   96-37340
                                                      CIP

Visit the Society's Web site at http://www.nationalgeographic.com or GO NATIONAL GEOGRAPHIC on CompuServe.